C000151481

Zach's
JOURNEY

Cormac O'Brolchain, Ph.D.

authorHOUSE®

AuthorHouse™ UK
1663 Liberty Drive
Bloomington, IN 47403 USA
www.authorhouse.co.uk
Phone: 0800.197.4150

© *2017 Cormac O'Brolchain, Ph.D.. All rights reserved.*

No part of this book may be reproduced, stored in a retrieval system, or transmitted by any means without the written permission of the author.

Published by AuthorHouse 05/18/2017

ISBN: 978-1-5246-8121-0 (sc)
ISBN: 978-1-5246-8122-7 (e)

Print information available on the last page.

This book is printed on acid-free paper.

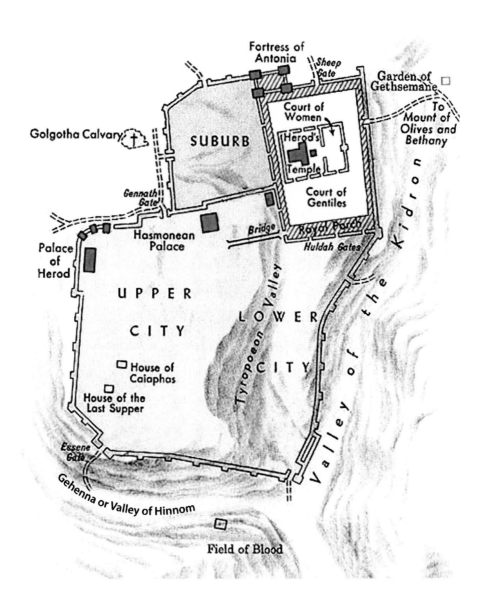

Fortress of
Antonia

*Sheep
Gate*

Garden of
Gethsemane

Golgotha Calvary ✝

SUBURB

Court of
Women

Herod's
Temple

To
Mount of
Olives and
Bethany

*Gennath
Gate*

Court of
Gentiles

Bridge

Hasmonean
Palace

Royal Porch

Huldah Gates

Palace
of
Herod

U P P E R

C I T Y

L O W E R

C I T Y

☐ House of
Caiaphas

☐
House of the
Last Supper

*Essene
Gate*

Gehenna or Valley of Hinnom

Field of Blood

Tyropoeon Valley

V a l l e y   o f   t h e   K i d r o n

PART 1

CHAPTER 1

He hated Roman soldiers and always asked his father why they had to be in his country. But of course deep down he knew why.

"It's all about money and power. They keep us under their thumbs so that they can steal our money to support their lavish lifestyles, and they call it taxes," Zachary, or Zach as he was usually called, had explained to his pal, Stephen. "These horrible men wander uninvited through our country. They are like nasty watch-dogs waiting to pounce and bite."

The Romans were never far away. And if there were any hint of a revolt, meaning any large gathering in one place, they could appear from nowhere. One moment they were not there, and then the sound of horses' hooves would fill the air and they would appear. The Romans seemed to have eyes everywhere. But they weren't the only ones.

"Antipas, you are just soft, unlike your father who would have quickly disposed of him."

"Darling Herodias, what has he done wrong?"

"He has told everybody that we are living in adultery and are a disgrace."

"But we *are* living in adultery, darling."

"Put him in jail – he will destroy your power and respect among the people."

"Of course he can't! But, just for you, I will send some men to bring him here so that you can talk with him yourself."

As Zach and his friend neared their destination, a group of Roman soldiers on horseback appeared and passed by them. When Zach saw their white tunics, their black and grey menacing armour, casting shadows as they passed, he almost started shouting and began looking for bricks to throw at them, but his pal managed to cool him down.

"Zach, all you see is a small group of soldiers, but be careful, there are always more not too far away. If a fight starts those people ahead of us could become involved and half an army will appear and you and I as well as those men, women and children could end up dead, and all because of the stone that you threw."

"You're right, Stephen. But every time I see them I feel this rush of blood inside me. Will we ever get rid of them?"

"Not anytime soon, I think."

"Are they going to see the prophet too?" Zach laughed contemptuously.

"I would say, not so much 'to see' as 'to watch'," Stephen said.

"I hope, Stephen, that they keep their swords, daggers and clubs to themselves when we are there or I will become involved."

"Trust in God, Zach, that that won't happen."

"Sure! And then what? Tell me, after all these decades, why are we still obeying these murderers and thieves. Think of all the money they take from us every year, money that could do so much good for our people. And what has God done to help us? Nothing!"

"Be patient, Zach."

Zach and Stephen were both fourteen years of age, not yet two years after their bar mitzvah, so their parents allowed them join a group from Capernaum that was going to Perea to see the prophet.

"My father told me that 'John the Baptist' is actually from a priestly family, but that he decided to spend his life preaching in the desert instead," said Stephen.

"Why, Stephen? What will he achieve out here in nowhere land?"

"Watch it!" continued Zach, as he touched the burning sand. "We had better make sure that our sandals don't fall off – the sand is boiling here. I can see why people wear a cover on their heads. This desert sun is as hot as a fire cooking fish."

"Zach, I am really looking forward to seeing him," Stephen said, smiling in expectation.

"Ouch! What a place, Stephen! John the Baptist must be mad to be living out here." Zach shook his head, he had just hit his toe off a stone.

"Zach, look! Is that the prophet... the one standing on his own, holding a large crook? I'm sure it is. He seems to be speaking to that group there. He looks so dark, so sun-burned." Stephen increased his pace.

"Are you surprised?" said Zach, "feel that sun... he must be crazy."

"Zach, look over there... the Roman soldiers who passed us."

The two pals looked for a while at the soldiers. The soldiers seemed to be quite content and were listening intently to John the Baptist.

"I suppose there is nothing we can do about them," Zach murmured.

"I don't think so. Let's ignore them. Look, here's a good spot. We can easily see John the Baptist from here." Stephen found a place beside a large rock that offered some shade. Some people were already there but there was enough space for the two pals. So they sat down and were quite close to the flowing Jordan River.

"Thanks a lot," Zach said gratefully, as the people made way for Stephen and himself.

"Zach, listen to that!" Stephen whispered. "We'll definitely be able to hear what John is saying. He has a really strong and clear voice."

"Yes, he has." A man sitting beside the two agreed.

But Zach found it nearly too hot out there in the desert, despite the shade of the rock. 'If the river wasn't here,' he told himself, 'it would be unbearable.'

As John the prophet spoke, Zach, instead of listening, was wondering where John actually lived. 'He surely couldn't live permanently out here in the desert, though at least he would have a water supply from the river, if he did,' mused Zach as he continued looking around for some house or tent. "No, it's not possible!" he muttered. "He could never survive in that lean-to beside those rocks."

"Yes, son, he does live there!" a stranger near Zach explained.

The stranger smiled at Zach's look of disbelief.

"Why does he live out here in a desert," asked Zach, "without friends and with practically nothing to eat?"

The stranger smiled.

Zach asked, "I have heard that the Baptiser lives on locusts and wild honey. Surely that can't be true?"

"It is, son," said the stranger, "and as to your former question as to why he would do such things, he is here to proclaim God's word to us. We are to change our ways and live better lives."

"It's amazing. You see I am not so interested in words and ideas," said Zach. "I like facts. I prefer examining facts. So if John lives on nothing then he can talk about it. Endless words but little or no action seems to be the way most of our society works."

The man nodded gently. So Zach began to study the Baptist's clothes — camel skin and a belt, nothing expensive, nothing for show.

"He is certainly different from anyone I have seen up to now," Zach muttered to himself.

As he looked around, he saw that, besides the soldiers, there were well-dressed people who looked as though they might come from Jerusalem. There were also priests in the crowd. But no matter who they were, they all seemed to be listening attentively to John who had just then asked for questions.

A man from a group of well-dressed people asked, "What must I do?"

John answered, "Whoever has two shirts must give one to the person who has none, and whoever has food must share it."

"Easier said than done," muttered Zach, as he listened to the exchange.

Then, to a small group of men who were booed when they asked a question that neither Zach nor Stephen could hear, John the Baptist said, "Don't collect more taxes than is legal."

"Zach, they are obviously local tax-collectors," said Stephen shaking his head in disapproval.

"I think you're right," said Zach. "The prophet should have condemned them outright for collecting taxes for the Romans or for our local, mad King and his wealthy friends."

The next question was from a soldier, who asked in Greek, "Have you anything to say to us?"

The crowd, seeing who asked the question, booed again. Some stood up and aggressively shook their fists at the soldier. A man beside Stephen cried "Scum!" But the disruption didn't last.

John replied in Greek. Both boys understood Greek, Zach because of his study and Stephen because it was his mother tongue.

"Don't take money from anyone by force or accuse anyone falsely," John the Baptist answered the soldier. "Be content with your pay."

The two friends looked at one another in amazement.

"Stephen," said Zach, "John is too soft on them, he should have told them to leave our country, preferably in chains."

Stephen said nothing but Zach knew that he agreed.

After some talk among themselves, the soldiers mounted their horses and rode off.

An onlooker then asked John, "Are you the Messiah who is supposed to come, the one who is to get rid of our enemies?"

John shook his head wearily, his long hair falling from side to side, his piercing eyes looking directly at the questioner.

"John looks like he is about to answer a silly child," observed Zach, amused.

"The man who will come after me," replied John the Baptist, "is much greater than I am. I am not good enough even to bend down and untie his sandals."

"What does that mean, Stephen?" asked Zach.

"I have no idea," said Stephen, "there must be someone who is coming, someone really special."

Just then some Pharisees and Sadducees, dressed immaculately and speaking with Jerusalem accents, began asking John questions. They said that their authority came from their father Abraham. "Isn't that a sufficient qualification?"

"You brood of vipers!" the Baptist answered, beating the sand with his stick. "Who warned you to flee from the wrath to come? Bear fruit worthy of penance... every tree that does not bear good fruit is cut down and thrown into the fire."

"That's more like it, Stephen," said Zach delighted. "John the Baptist is not interested in just words, or posturing, but in doing good deeds. But why was he so tough on them and not so on the Roman soldiers?" Zach was now looking at John, trying to understand.

"They don't seem too pleased with the Baptiser's reaction," said Stephen as he looked at the faces of the Pharisees and Sadducees from Jerusalem.

"But listen!" Zach said, nudging Stephen. "John is now criticising Herod Antipas for his wedding to his brother's wife, Herodias. I've heard that he has criticised them before. That certainly won't go down well. My father says the Herods are clever but are also half-mad and very dangerous. He told me that Antipas' father had his wife, mother-in-law and two sons killed for not supporting him."

Stephen was stunned. "Are you serious, Zach?" he said. "I did hear that he killed a whole lot of students and two professors for removing a pagan symbol from the Temple. But to kill his own family – he's definitely mad, and dangerous... Zach, you will have to agree that John is fearless and trusts in God." He smiled as he spoke, knowing that his pal Zach had difficulty believing in God.

"I wouldn't chance taking on the authorities, especially the Herod family. I wonder if John is wise," mused Zach.

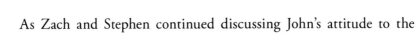

As Zach and Stephen continued discussing John's attitude to the various groups, they heard him offering to baptise those who wished to confess their wrongdoings and change their ways.

"What do you think, Stephen, will we go? I am really not that religious," said Zach looking at Stephen – half-hoping that Stephen would not get involved.

"Why not, Zach?" said Stephen. "I'd like to get help to become a better person, to improve my attitude to life."

Zach was hesitant, but then the two pals waded into the water, following some others who had come from Capernaum. As they stood in the water they watched carefully and saw that John spoke for a little while to each person before baptising them.

'What will he say to me?' Zach wondered, now considering changing his mind. 'Maybe, I'll let Stephen receive baptism for both of us' – but it was too late.

"What is your name, young man?"

In front of Zach stood this tall, strong, if hungry-looking, man with wild hair and a long beard that was floating in the water. His deep, penetrating eyes looked straight into Zach's. All of a sudden, totally un-expectedly, Zach was overcome with emotion and fright, tears filling his eyes. He barely knew what to do or say.

"My name is Zachary bar Zebedee, Sir," he stuttered.

6

"Zachary, do you want to be baptised?" John smiled at him but seemed to leave the door open for him to say no.

"Do I?" replied Zach, trying to control all sorts of strange feelings, "Yes! Oh yes, please."

"So, Zachary," John the Baptist continued, "are you sorry for all your wrong doings, your sins?"

"Yes, Sir. Yes, I am." He wasn't sure why he was sure.

"Zachary, God has forgiven you all your sins. But know this — you may have difficulties at this time believing in the Lord God but he has great work for you to do. Have courage, then, and never give up your search for intimacy with God."

Zach stared at John the Baptist, eyes wide open in fright. How did John know about his lack of belief? He was utterly speechless for a moment, but then, somehow, he was able to reply.

"I'll try my best," he said, though not really knowing what John meant by 'intimacy with God' or if there was a God at all.

John smiled again, and with his strong hands he submerged Zach under the water, water that Zach imagined had come down from the pure snowy peaks of Israel. As Zach resurfaced, frozen and needing air, his hair doused, his hands almost blue, John said a blessing and then gently motioned for Zach to make way for Stephen.

Zach never found out what John said to Stephen, nor did he tell Stephen what John said to him, but somehow they both became more mature and focused from that moment on.

It all happened so suddenly the following day.

"What's that noise Stephen?" asked Zach, as he stretched himself outside the tent, the beginning of a new day.

"It sounds like horses," said Stephen, hurrying out of the tent. "Look at that dust cloud over there. There must be a fair number of them." At first it was just a cloud of dusty sand but then they appeared – ten horses racing towards the river – but only nine riders.

"They're King Herod's men," Stephen said. "I've seen them once before. They are a scary group."

Without regard for anyone, the soldiers rode through the place where the crowd had spent the night. Everyone was trying to jump out of their way. There was screaming and shouting... mothers with children, men, some very frightened, others waving aggressively. It was horrific. One child got a terrible blow from the leg of the lead horse as her mother tried to grab her, narrowly escaping death herself.

When the soldiers reached the place where John the Baptist was, three dismounted, while the other six sat looking threateningly at the furious crowd. The three dismounted soldiers began to beat John with clubs, and anyone who tried to shield him. But the crowd hadn't a chance of stopping Herod's men. The soldiers on the horses had their swords and clubs ready to be used if anyone tried anything further. There was no doubt that they would use their weapons given the slightest reason.

"Is there anything we can do, Stephen?" Zach whispered angrily.

"I don't think so, unless we want to put our lives at risk trying," Stephen replied.

After the beating, John was tied up. He was only half-conscious and there was blood oozing from his head. Without sympathy, the brutish, arrogant soldiers flung him over a horse, and tied him to it. A few bystanders attempted once more to help John, but they were viciously clubbed.

Then, with an angry shout, the leader of the soldiers kicked his horse and as suddenly as they had come they had disappeared in a cloud of dust, carrying with them, the tied-up, half-conscious John the Baptist.

When the soldiers were at a safe distance, where they wouldn't consider returning to make a point, everyone shouted after them. Some were hysterical. Zach was furious, his eyes half-closed, his head working out possible ways to get back at them at some future date.

"Stephen, Herod's soldiers are as ruthless and as bad as any of the Roman legions that live here," Zach spoke quietly.

"So much for justice," Stephen said, holding back his rage. "The Herod dynasty marches on, trampling on anyone who they think disagrees with them. I wonder whether, when we are older Zach, we will be able to do anything to stop these dreadful people."

Chapter 2

"Stephen," said Zach. "I think something very bad has happened since we were away. The welcoming party looks very upset."

Both the mothers ran to their sons and gave them big hugs. Zach's mother was in tears.

"Mum, what is wrong?" Zach asked. "Is someone dead? Was there a drowning in the sea? Where is James? Is Ruth all right?"

"No, Zach, everything is fine. Thank God you are both safely home."

There was silence as Zach's mum got her thoughts together. Stephen and Zach became very worried.

Then Zach's mother spoke.

"We heard of Herod's capture of John the Baptist and the clashes with Herod's soldiers and all the injuries and the two deaths. We thought that you both might have been involved. Thank God, again, that you are both home, safe from harm."

Stephen and Zach shook their heads in thanks that nothing disastrous had happened to their families, and that they had done nothing to Herod's soldiers. They had seen the beatings and a man cut with a sword but hadn't known that there were also some deaths.

Zach's father and two brothers James and John arrived just then.

"We have no idea where they took John the Baptist," Zach said.

Zach's father spoke. "The prophet has been taken to Machaerus."

Zach and Stephen were amazed that Zach's father could be so well informed of what happened.

"Is that one of Herod's fortresses?" Zach asked his dad.

"Yes... it is." Zebedee nodded his head slowly, obviously aware of the meaning of what he said. Looking at him, the two pals decided not to pursue the issue any further.

With that the whole group went to the Zebedee house where the two mothers had prepared a meal. The two friends were very hungry and were delighted to sit and tell their families what had happened on their trip. When they had finished their accounts Zach's brother, John, asked if they had seen Yeshua bar Joseph in the desert.

"No, I have never seen him," responded Zach, "but I did hear you and James mention him. Did you see him, Stephen?"

Stephen's mind had wandered. He was thinking of how lucky he and Zach were to have done nothing when both the Roman and Herod's soldiers were in Perea. "Sorry, Zach?" said Stephen.

Zach smiled, "Did you see Yeshua bar Joseph from Nazareth at Perea," he repeated.

"I don't think so. You and I were together all the time. We did see many people and maybe we did see him, but just didn't know who he was. Who is Yeshua bar Joseph?" Stephen asked.

"Well," Zach's brother John continued, "Yeshua is someone whom James and I have known for some time. He has been here for short visits in the last few years and particularly recently. It seems that he asked John the Baptist to baptise him but John refused."

"Why would the prophet do that?" Zach interrupted. "Unless of course Yeshua wasn't sorry for his sins."

John smiled and continued, "The Baptist said to Yeshua, 'No! Rather you baptise me.'"

"Zach and I," Stephen said, remembering a statement of the prophet, "did hear the prophet say, 'The man who will come after me is much greater than I am. I am not good enough even to bend down and untie his sandals.' – or something like that."

"Those were the exact words, Stephen," Zach agreed. "so maybe he was talking about Yeshua?"

"I'm sure he was. Yeshua is rather special," John added.

Zach noted the way his brother replied. 'The man he was talking about, Yeshua bar Joseph, must be very special indeed,' Zach thought.

At that stage both of the pals wondered if there was more to this questioning than they understood.

"John the Baptist is undoubtedly special himself," John continued in a very measured way, "but Yeshua is just different. James and I, along with

Andrew and his brother Simon, have never met anyone like him. In fact, I gather that when Yeshua came out of the water after John had baptised him, a dove appeared over Yeshua's head and a voice said, 'You are my beloved son, I am pleased with you.'"

"A voice in the desert? John... where did the voice come from?" Zach asked. He wondered if his brother was being serious.

"What do *you* think, Zach?" their mother joined in.

"Don't tell me it was from God!" Zach now realised that what John was saying had been discussed already.

Their mother smiled as did his brothers, James and John, but Zach's father gave him a knowing wink, as if to say, 'I'm on your side, Zach.'

It was late, so they soon finished their meal and when Stephen and his family went home Zach gave his mother an affectionate hug and said goodnight. Both of the pals were totally exhausted.

Just before Zach fell asleep, as he thought about what John and his mother had said, he felt somehow that life seemed changed at home. It was so different to hear his brothers talking about some stranger called Yeshua bar Joseph in such glowing terms. Yes, that was very unusual. 'James and John,' he thought to himself, 'and of course my mum, are balanced people, not easily impressed. Surely, James, my Dad's right-hand man, won't do anything foolish. No, he understands real life. And neither will John. He's too smart to get involved with prophets and do-gooders. Look at John the Baptist. He is obviously a very good, impressive man – but isn't very practical. What did the prophet gain from criticising Herod? Nothing! That's not the way to live life.' Then, content that life would not be all that different when he woke up next morning, Zach fell asleep.

As the fishing was good over the next number of weeks, Zach hardly noticed the days passing. Life seemed nearly back to normal again and the discussion on the evening of his return and the wonderful and terrible happenings in the desert were becoming distant memories. However, he did still think a great deal about the baptism and the words John the prophet spoke to him, 'You may have difficulties now in believing in the Lord God, but he has great work for you to do. Have courage, then, and never give up your search for intimacy with God.'

As he pulled in the nets, sorted the fish, mended the nets and helped his dad prepare the fish for sale, he often heard those words going around in his head.

He also told another very good friend of his what had happened. Her name was Ruth. She was the daughter of Jairus, the leader of the town's synagogue, and his wife Esther. Zach always confided in her. She somehow understood issues in a different way to him. And more often than not, she was nearer to the truth than he was, at least that is what he believed. She also was able to keep secrets. Zach often felt that he would have been quite lost without her. Among other things she was also very attractive and bright. Zach was especially happy when she supported John the Baptist's view that God had work for him to do, even though she knew well that Zach's belief in God was shaky at best. She was a year younger than him but, as he had confessed to Stephen, "She is probably more mature than either of us, even though I will never admit that to her."

Around eight weeks after the visit to John the Baptist in the desert, Zach, after a night's fishing with his brother John, noticed a stranger walking along the shore. He was about five feet ten inches tall, which was taller than most people Zach had ever met. He had long, dark hair and a black beard. As Zach looked at him, he felt that there was something about the stranger that was somehow different. He couldn't say what that 'something' was precisely.

"Look, John! Who is that man over there?" he asked.

John looked up from his work on the nets and immediately his face lit up.

"That is the man I was telling you about."

"You mean Yeshua bar Joseph?"

"Yes, that is Yeshua bar Joseph from Nazareth."

As he was speaking John quickly motioned to the other workmen to take over from him. Then, putting his hand on Zach's shoulder, he shouted across to his other brother who was still clearing up.

"James, he's here!"

James looked at the stranger who had now reached Simon bar Jona's house, and quickly finished what he was doing. He jumped out of the boat and joined John and Zach.

"John, look! He's talking to Simon and Andrew. It seems as though both Simon and Andrew have agreed."

"Has Simon finished the extension to his house?" John asked.

"Yes, two days ago," James replied.

Zach was lost at this stage. He had no idea what his brothers were talking about.

"What is this all about?" he asked.

James turned to Zach and with a smile explained, "Zach, both John and I are taking a short break from fishing. We are joining Yeshua in a project he has organised."

"What?" Zach couldn't believe what he was hearing. Consternation was written all over his face. If ever there was a fisherman it was James. He got on so well in the business. If there were any problems their father, Zebedee, always turned to James. If James decided that something should be done, it was done. Nobody would argue with him. All the workmen respected James. With him the family business had a bright future.

Just as he was finished mulling it all over in his head he saw Yeshua, with both Simon and Andrew, coming towards their jetty.

"Peace to you. You must be Zach!" Yeshua said with his deep, clear voice.

"Peace to you, Sir... Yes, I'm Zach."

"It is good to meet you, Zach. Your family has been telling me good things about you."

"Have they?" Zach looked at James and John and his mum, and wondered when they had been speaking to this stranger about him. But then, recovering from the questioning in his mind, he replied, "And, my brothers have been telling me great things about you, Sir."

Yeshua smiled, and then greeted all the family who by that time had gathered to meet 'the stranger', Yeshua. When Yeshua had greeted everyone individually, including all the workers, Zebedee's wife, Salome, said, "Can I invite you all in for some food?"

"It would be an honour," Yeshua replied, "but James and John, Simon, Andrew and I need a few moments together. We will be with you right away."

Zach and his parents headed for the house. But when Zach opened the door and looked inside, there, all arranged, was a meal for the exact number that were outside including Simon, Andrew and Yeshua, and all the workers. It was only then that he fully understood that his parents were well aware of everything that was happening.

"Dad, why didn't you tell me about all this?" he asked, with a face that was supposed to say 'I am not a child any more.'

"Nothing was certain until a few weeks ago," Zebedee explained, "and since you were still upset about John the Baptist we didn't want to worry you any more than was necessary."

What could he say? It was true. He was pretty disturbed by what happened in the desert and he realised that if he had known that this change was about to break into his life he might have caused trouble at home. He shrugged his shoulders, but was not at all happy. Yet he had to admit to himself that Yeshua bar Joseph seemed to have something special about him.

After awhile Yeshua and the others came in. Zach had rarely seen his brothers so happy. He then wondered if he too might join this happy group.

As he considered that, Yeshua looked across the table and spoke to him.

"Zach, as I said, your brothers have told me a great deal about you."

'What now?' thought Zach. His brothers were looking at him and smiling.

"They told me that you would be well able to fill in for them when they are away from Capernaum from time to time. Your dad agrees too. What do you think, Zach?"

What could he say?

CHAPTER 3

"Did you hear what's happening?" Zach asked his friends when he saw them the next day.

"What is happening?" Ruth and Stephen hadn't seen him so upset for some time.

"Do you mean about Yeshua and his new project?" It was Joseph, the fourth member of the group, the young brother of Simon and Andrew, who spoke.

"I'm lost here," Stephen said, "is there something new happening in the town?"

"I had my suspicions," Joseph said. "Simon and Andrew had visited John the Baptist a while ago and when they came home they were talking about Yeshua. Seemingly the prophet introduced them to Yeshua. It was just after Yeshua's baptism. Then, when you, Zach, and Stephen were away with John in the desert, Yeshua came to visit our house and stayed for two days. James and John also came over to us and there was a great discussion. I didn't stay and listen to their discussion but it went on for at least half the day. Yeshua, it seems, has a plan for a better world."

"Plans are one thing, but making them work is something else," Zach interrupted.

"Oh Zach! Wouldn't it be great if our lives could be better?" It was Ruth who said this. "You are smart, Zach, and like your brother John and Stephen, you study a lot. But you need to open your heart."

"Maybe you're right, Ruth," Zach agreed.

"I don't know much, not being one who studies a great deal," Joseph continued, "but from meeting Yeshua I believe that he is someone who might be able to do something."

As the four walked along together they discussed what was happening and what it might mean for their lives. Firstly, Simon was a widower and his family, including his mother-in-law, would need to agree to this change. He owned his boats and of course the family could continue the business, but it was a huge change for both him and Andrew.

"Joseph, you will probably have to do double work. Did you agree to this change?" Stephen asked.

"How could I disagree? Anyway I like being busy and we've taken on two new helpers. Also, my brothers must have great belief in Yeshua to just get up and go with him. Simon told me that Yeshua had said he would make himself and Andrew 'fishers of people'." Joseph laughed, as he imagined himself pulling up nets from the sea with people inside them.

"What a crazy idea!" Zach laughed, picking up the mood from Joseph.

"Simon also said," continued Joseph, "that he and Andrew weighed it up and are convinced that it's the right thing to do at this time."

"Good for them," said Ruth, then added, "It isn't for ever, Zach, only for the length of the project. They'll be back soon, stronger and more eager than ever."

They were seriously underestimating the changes to come.

In Galilee at that time it was taken for granted that Satan, the chief and most terrible demon, with hordes of other demons, roamed around, particularly at night, attempting to harm and destroy people. Zach and his pals had often discussed the presence of demons. The night before this Sabbath meeting in the synagogue they had actually done so at length.

"There were many times when I was younger," admitted Zach, "that I ran home in terror, having heard or seen something that I couldn't understand. I only felt safe when I saw James or John, or of course my parents. Even at night in bed when I was around five or six, I remember being so scared that I covered my head with a blanket and hoped that the sun would come up and get rid of the demons. At those times listening to my own breath or heartbeat was nearly enough to make me panic, not knowing whether it was my breath or the breath of a demon, or whether it was my heartbeat or a demon walking towards me... thump, thump."

His pals nodded, able to relate to the experience.

"It was, and sometimes is still, the exact same with me," Stephen agreed. "That's why in our house we leave a light burning all night to give some feeling of safety. I feel a little safer these days like you, Zach, but I have to admit that it wouldn't take much to make me feel scared."

"Nor me, Stephen," nodded Zach.

"And here I was thinking that I was the only one of us scared out of my mind at the thought of demons," added Ruth. "I just hope I never ever meet one."

The next time they saw Yeshua was at the town synagogue on the Sabbath and the four 'fishers of people' were with him. Zach mightn't have gone to the synagogue except that he had heard Yeshua would be there.

That day Yeshua took his turn to read the Scriptures. When he had finished he spoke to the people who were gathered there. Everyone listened very carefully and many were won over by the personal authority he showed. Yeshua stressed that what people thought in their heads mattered a great deal, but, 'You only know a tree by its fruits,' he explained.

Zach, who sat with his dad, murmured "This all makes sense, but what can we really do in our downtrodden society?" His dad smiled.

"What is that?" Stephen whispered.

Zach, Stephen and Joseph, as well as Zach's dad, Zebedee, all looked towards the back of the synagogue. A young man, whom they had never seen before, was shouting. He looked really terrifying. His eyes were a menacing red, his pupils were small black dots. They were angry eyes. His face was one big, ferocious grimace, full of aggression, his hair wild, his skin a deathly grey. He was half-spitting as he spoke, "What do you want with us, Yeshua of Nazareth? Are you here to destroy us? I know who you are – you are God's holy messenger."

"Did you hear that?" said Joseph in a fearful whisper.

Panic was rising in the synagogue. People were cowering and muttering in groups all around, particularly near to the young man. Zach was looking towards the door for an escape route, but the man whom he now thought was possessed by a demon, was between their group and the door.

Then a deep, clear and commanding voice said, "Be quiet, and come out of the man!" It was Yeshua.

Immediately the young man let out a terrible scream, like birds fighting over a fish. Zach was worried about Ruth, who would be in a terrible state behind the screen with the women.

'How will she deal with this?' he thought anxiously.

Then the young man's body started to shake and he began frothing at the mouth. He tried to stay standing, staggering from pillar to pillar, with everyone quickly getting out of his way. There were screams from the women's area and even from some of the men. Then suddenly the young man, exhausted, sat down on a bench and with very tired eyes looked around the synagogue. He didn't seem to know where he was.

"The poor man," Zach whispered, "he is completely confused."

"I agree, but I still won't go near him," Stephen whispered back.

Yeshua, however, was now beside the young man, helping him to stand up. The four 'fishers of people' were also close by. When the young man finally stood up Yeshua put his arms around him. The man's father, who was weeping, was also beside his son and he too wrapped him in his arms.

"Thank you, Yeshua bar Joseph," said the man's father. "For so long my son has been like he was this morning. How can I ever thank you enough?"

"Your son will be fine now," said Yeshua calmly, "but he will need some rest to fully recover his strength," and smiling, Yeshua left the synagogue.

"What do you make of that, Zach?" Stephen asked.

"I don't know what's happening," Zach replied.

"You have just seen an exorcism," Zach's dad, Zebedee, explained. "Unlike others, who use all sorts of prayers and rituals, Yeshua just commanded the demon to leave the young man's body and it did."

Zach, Stephen and Joseph were shocked. Life had become so different.

"Yeshua is special," Zebedee quietly concluded.

As they made their way out of the synagogue Ruth appeared from the women's area and said, "Wasn't that really frightening? At least I was behind the screen. You must have been terrified. But what a gift they got from Yeshua!"

"You're right, Ruth," said Zach. "The boy's dad must have been living a nightmare. Imagine it, every day to have to look after your demon-possessed son."

"I will never forget today," Stephen added.

Some people passed by. "I hope this craftsman from Nazareth leaves us alone," they muttered.

"And he cured on the Sabbath. Isn't that forbidden?"

It wasn't long before the whole of Galilee had heard about what happened in the synagogue that morning.

Yeshua, after leaving the seriously disrupted synagogue, went to Simon and Andrew's house where James and John joined them. A midday meal is normal on the Sabbath. However, when Yeshua and the four 'fishers of people' were approaching Simon's house, Simon explained, "Yeshua, you didn't see Deborah, my mother-in-law, at the synagogue because unfortunately she is down with a burning fever. They are so common around here."

"Simon, let's go and see her," Yeshua suggested.

Deborah's room was dark when they entered it and it was only with difficulty that they could see her lying on her bed. Her face was pale and drawn and her hair and clothes were covered in sweat. She had a rasping cough and tried to tell Simon to keep away.

"Simon, you shouldn't have come. You will only get sick too. It's bad enough for one of us to be sick."

"Yeshua is here, Deborah. He would like to visit you."

Yeshua quietly went over to Deborah.

John later explained to Zach and his friends that, "Yeshua didn't use the normal rituals and blessings that our Rabbis use. He just quietly and reverently, took Deborah's hand, closed his eyes and prayed for a few moments. Then, like the sun coming out from behind a cloud and filling the room with sunshine, the fever left her. Her dizziness and coughing stopped and the pallor of her face was replaced by its usual healthy colour.

Wiping a tear from her eye, she thanked Yeshua and whooshed Simon and Yeshua out of her room. Then, a few minutes later she appeared, dressed in her Sabbath best, and set about preparing the meal. All the others were summarily dismissed from their duties. You all know, from meeting her, that there was no use arguing. She was obviously back to her normal self."

Joseph smiled and nodded.

"The meal, I gather, was delicious," Zach said.

"She is a great cook," Joseph agreed.

In accordance with the Jewish law, 'when three stars are visible the Sabbath officially ends.' At precisely that moment crowds from the town arrived at Simon's house. Many of them were sick, and some were possessed by demons.

"This is not fair on Yeshua, expecting him to work into the night curing people. Why won't they wait until tomorrow?" Ruth asked, annoyed at the lack of concern for Yeshua.

"Most of us think only of ourselves," Stephen suggested, nodding in agreement with Ruth.

"I hope our brothers will be able to control these crowds, Zach," said the ever-practical Joseph.

"Look at all those people shouting or snarling. They seem like caged animals," Stephen said, having experienced nothing like it before.

"And Yeshua is telling the demons to go. What a sight!" said Ruth.

"Ruth, look over there at that young girl." It was Zach who spoke. His face showed that he was quite horrified.

The girl he was looking at was tearing at her tangled hair with her long-nailed fingers, spitting, trying to break free from her father's firm grip and rubbing her hand across her drooling mouth.

"She is only a little older than me." Ruth was aghast.

"Luckily her dad is strong," said Zach. "He'll be able to make sure that she doesn't get out of control."

When finally the girl and her parents reached Yeshua, she let out a prolonged, high-pitched, terrible shriek. Ruth put her hands to her ears. It sounded as if she had been slashed with a double-edged sword across her throat. But she was immediately cured by Yeshua.

"Zach, this is terrifying," Stephen muttered.

"This must be as bad as it gets," Joseph said.

Little did they know.

"If this is what it is going to be like for Simon, Andrew and my two brothers, they are going to have a really tough time," Zach remarked. After four hours all the people had gone.

Once again, that night Zach couldn't get to sleep, thinking of all the cures and the demons that Yeshua cast out. He also, for some reason, remembered something that happened to him eight years earlier. It concerned a boy called Timothy who was a friend of his brother James.

Eight years earlier, when Zach was only six years old, he had come into the front room of his house to see James there.

"James, where is Timothy?" he asked but James became very distressed, not knowing what to say to his younger brother.

"Zach, he is ill," James said, as if people often become ill and it was nothing to worry about.

"I hope he gets better soon. I love when he comes to see us," Zach said.

James turned away, wiped tears from his eyes, and left the room. Zach had never seen him cry before.

"Where is Timothy?" Zach whispered to his mother. Salome pretended not to hear him. She was a wonderful cook and had just finished preparing some lovely food.

"Who's that for?" Zach asked.

"Zach," she smiled, "it's for Timothy."

"But, Mum, James told me he is ill," replied Zach.

"He is, so I am bringing him some special food," Salome smilingly replied.

"Can I go with you, Mum?" Zach asked with enthusiasm.

"Better not, Zach, he lives a long, long way away. I'll be back in about four hours or so," Salome answered, patting him on the head.

As she was going out the door, with her parcel of food, he said goodbye and then pretended to stay in the house. But when she had rounded the bend at the top of the road he followed her, hiding anytime he thought she might look backwards, but she never did.

After some miles Salome went into what Zach knew was Timothy's house. When she entered he crept up and looked in the window to see if he could see Timothy. But Timothy didn't seem to be there. Only his mother and Timothy's mother were there. At that stage Zobo, Timothy's dog, appeared and began barking. Zach, who knew Zobo well, motioned to him to stop barking, which he did as he sidled up to Zach wagging his tail. Zach gave Zobo a big hug.

"And who have we here?" Timothy's mother appeared at the door. On seeing who it was she smiled, but Zach noticed that there was a tear in her eye.

21

"Zach, I thought you were at home," Salome, appearing just beside her, announced in a tone that showed her disapproval of her son taking it on himself to follow her.

"I really wanted to see Timothy," he said, realising that his mother was annoyed with him. "He is such great fun when he comes to our house. And we are all very fond of him, especially James."

There was no answer from either woman.

"I'll bring it myself," Zach's mother said.

"No, Salome, it is too terrible."

Zach was confused. 'What is terrible?' he asked himself.

"Don't be silly," Salome smiled and then turned to Zach. "Zach, you stay here with Timothy's mother until I return. I'll be back in twenty to thirty minutes."

That was one thing Zach did not want to do, but he said nothing. His mother then left with the special food while Timothy's mother waved goodbye.

When Zach's mother was gone a distance, Timothy's mother kindly gave Zach a few games to keep him occupied.

"Will you be all right?" she said with a smile that seemed to Zach the kind of smile that you give when you are really trying not to cry.

"I'm fine, don't worry about me," Zach answered with great gusto. But when she had gone back inside Zach ran to the end of the small garden of the house and, climbing under the fence, followed his mother. Salome had already gone a good distance but, since Zach was a fast runner for his age and since she was only walking, he soon caught up on her. However, in case she would see him and become angry again, he kept both sufficiently near to make sure he didn't lose her and, at the same time, sufficiently far away to avoid detection. Sometimes he thought his mother would look backwards so he hid quickly in pieces of brush, but she never did.

After what seemed an age, Salome reached an outcrop with a large cave in it. 'Is she going to the caves?' Zach asked himself. 'Surely my mother will not go there, there could be wolves living there.'

He nearly shouted after his mother but at the last moment he saw that she was not going into the cave. Instead, she had put down the food she was bringing and began singing a line from a song. She sang it three times. Zach didn't know what she was doing. But then it became clear. He saw the once tall, strong and athletic Timothy appear out of the caves. Zach hardly recognised him. There Timothy was, standing with his face half-covered. He looked so much older and his face had all sorts of sores on it, and his fingers were black. He also had a red lump on his nose. Zach then realised that he was looking at a leper. Timothy was a leper. Zach froze. He found it hard to breathe and felt dizzy. But somehow, with much effort, he calmed himself down. Then he saw Salome wave to Timothy and point to the food. He realised that she was not going to go near Timothy and risk getting leprosy too. Salome was about to leave so he quickly left his hiding spot and ran as fast as he could back to the house.

Zach was lucky that he got over the small hill that led to the rocks before his mother could see him. He ran and ran, and when he finally arrived back at Timothy's house, he sat outside the door crying for his friend. Zobo came to greet him and Zach held him tightly and confided what he had seen. The dog seemed to understand his sadness and licked his face.

To Zach's amazement, it seemed that Timothy's mother hadn't realised that he had been away, since, when he got back his breath, dried his eyes and went into the house, she came out of her bedroom rubbing her eyes.

"Is everything all right, Zach?" she said gently, her hair tossed and her eyes red.

"I was wondering if I could have a little water," he said.

"Of course, child," she answered, happy that this was all he needed.

Zach realised that she must have been crying the whole time he had been away.

CHAPTER 4

Zach was very upset when John came into his room and told him that Yeshua was missing. No one knew why or where he had gone. Zach felt as if someone had died.

'But I have only known Yeshua for a week,' he told himself. 'So why am I so upset?'

Getting up quickly, he joined James and John and the others looking for Yeshua. They went to every house in the town. But there was no sign of him. Was he hiding? And why would he hide? It didn't look good at all. Stephen joined Zach in the search and together they tried to think of anywhere he could have been hidden in the town if he had been captured by evil people.

"Maybe he was beaten up like John and taken away when we were asleep?" Stephen suggested.

"Could a demon have taken him, I wonder?" Zach asked, thinking of the possibility that the demons were getting revenge.

"No Zach! He tells them where to go, not the other way around," Stephen replied.

After some time searching, however, Simon and Andrew finally found Yeshua at prayer in the desert.

"Yeshua, everyone is looking for you," Simon said with a questioning look on his face.

Yeshua just smiled. "Simon, it is time for us to move to other towns and villages," he said.

The following day, the four 'fishers of people', together with Yeshua, set off towards the West of Galilee.

Their trip lasted about twelve weeks and Yeshua taught in synagogues, cured many who were ill, and cast out demons.

————— ┼┼┼┼┼┼ —————

One morning, Stephen came running to Zach's house. Joseph and Ruth were also there with Zach.

"Yeshua and the four are just a few miles away," Stephen explained.

"Will we go and see how they are getting on?" Zach asked.

"Why not?" said Stephen.

As Zach, Stephen, Ruth and Joseph, now called 'the gang' by some, walked the few miles to see Yeshua, Zach began telling his pals the story of his visit to Timothy when he was six.

"How could God allow such a disease to attack a good person like Timothy?" Zach asked his friends. "God either didn't care about Timothy or maybe God doesn't exist!"

"Are you still unsure of God's existence?" Stephen said looking into his eyes, wondering if this was just an act Zach was putting on.

"Zach, how can we know what a good God is when we only have our little brains? Do we even understand the lives of the fish in our sea of Galilee?" Ruth asked.

"Of course we don't understand the lives of the fish," Zach agreed.

"Do we understand the workings of even one fish?" Stephen asked.

"Probably not, but that doesn't take away from the horror of Timothy's sickness," Zach countered.

"Zach, I feel the same," said Ruth, "but when I look at the stars and the mountains and the Sea of Galilee, I realise that we are small and insignificant. So for the moment, why don't we listen to Yeshua and see if things will become clearer for us?"

"Yes, 'for the moment', we all probably agree on that," said Zach smiling at Ruth and realising that he had met his match.

After some time they reached an opening in a fairly deserted area and there, about two hundred yards away, were Yeshua and the four walking towards them.

"There's Yeshua and our brothers," Joseph announced.

But just then, Stephen noticed a movement in a bush near Yeshua.

"Look! Is that a leper in the bushes, moving towards Yeshua?" Stephen asked with horror.

"It couldn't be," Ruth suggested, but she was worried. "You know that lepers have to stay away from people and shout, 'Unclean! Unclean!'"

"I think it is a leper, Ruth, and I know he shouldn't be there. But the question is, what will Yeshua do now?" It was Joseph who spoke.

Simon, at that stage, had raised his voice and was telling the leper to go away.

"It's all right Simon. Don't worry," Yeshua quietly said, putting his hand on Simon's arm. The four moved away and left Yeshua to meet the man on his own.

The leper's eyes were sunk into his head. His hair was wild. He had a beard that seemed to cover up all sorts of sores, and his finger nails were long and, like the rest of his body, unwashed for some considerable time.

With arms outstretched, the leper knelt down in front of Yeshua, bowed down and with a barely audible, hoarse voice said, "If you want to, you can make me clean."

Yeshua's companions were shocked. So were the gang.

But if that was bad, what happened next was worse. Yeshua, seemingly unafraid of getting the disease himself, and ignoring all the laws concerning leprosy, touched the leper on his head as if giving him a blessing.

"I do want to. Be clean!" Yeshua said to the leper.

Then, to everyone's utter disbelief, the leper's arm began to heal, his face began to lose the nodes that were festering there, his hands began to re-form, and, before they had time to take it all in, they saw the 'cleansed' leper kneeling in front of Yeshua, now perfectly healed. He was young, tall, athletic and handsome.

Helped by Yeshua, the leper stood up. He looked at his hands and then felt his face and body and arms. He was cured. Overcome with emotion, he looked again at Yeshua and embraced him. But before the leper could say anything, Yeshua spoke.

"Tell nobody that I cured you," he said, "but go to the priests to get a certificate of healing so that you can rejoin society and your own people."

Zach stared at the cured leper and was suddenly lost for words. "I don't believe it – I don't believe it," he spluttered. "It's Timothy!"

James, like Zach, had also recognised the leper and was walking briskly towards him.

"Timothy! Timothy! Is it you?" James asked, as he gave his friend an emotional hug. Tears were pouring down his face. In silence the two friends held one another.

Ruth was crying openly, while Stephen and Joseph were pretending merely to rub their eyes. Zach went over to Timothy to welcome him back.

Stephen, who had heard Yeshua asking Timothy not to tell anyone, turned to Ruth and Joseph. "No doubt Yeshua realises that if Timothy tells others about his cure, all the lepers in Galilee might start following Yeshua through the towns and villages," he said. "It could cause chaos."

But Timothy, of course, was overcome with happiness, and could not resist telling 'just a few' friends about the cure. And who could blame him?

Zach, meanwhile, wondered how Timothy's mother would feel. He already saw how James' joy was close to ecstatic. But for a mother who had to worry about her son every day for years, how incredible her joy would be. What a gift Yeshua had given them.

But as expected, Timothy spreading the news to 'just a few' grew to 'a few more' and then to 'many' and before long to 'nearly everyone'. And life became extremely difficult for Yeshua. From then on he had to avoid going into populated areas. He generally stayed outside the towns, in lonely places. But of course even that became pointless. The crowds found Yeshua wherever he went. Ruth put it well when she said, "Yeshua has changed places with Timothy."

CHAPTER 5

"Zach, are you coming up to our house? Yeshua is there now." Joseph was looking in through the door of Zach's house.

"Sure. What about Ruth and Stephen?" Zach said, quickly putting away what he was doing.

"We'll ask them to join us," Joseph smiled.

So Joseph and Zach were off. Ruth was already up and ready to go. As they left Ruth's house they met Stephen who was on his way to meet them.

"Let's go in the back door," Joseph suggested. "There is a little alcove beside the main room that will be a great place to see what is going on. Lots of people have already arrived."

The group ran quickly and, on reaching the house, they made their way through the cooking area into a small alcove. There were four little cushions already there. Joseph had planned it well.

"You're a genius, Joseph," Stephen remarked. "We can see everything that's happening from here. It's perfect."

After a short delay Yeshua began speaking. He spoke calmly, with his deep resonant voice, and every word was clear. He described a 'kingdom' where people loved one another, cared for each other, helped one another, forgave one another and respected one another. The people gathered there listened, laughed, pondered and loved every minute with him. Then he spoke of a house. Yeshua said, "Anyone who hears these words of mine and obeys them is like a wise man who built his house on rock. The rain poured down, the rivers flooded, and the wind blew hard against that house. But it did not fall, because it was built on rock. But anyone who hears these words of mine and does not obey them is like a foolish man who built his house on sand. The rain poured down, the rivers flooded, the wind blew hard against that house, and it fell. And what a terrible fall that was."

"He is so easy to listen to," Joseph said.

"I love all the stories he uses to explain his message," Ruth added.

"He paints a wonderful picture of 'The Kingdom of God'. I'm not too keen on kingdoms, however. Look at Rome and their world-wide empire and then the Herods and their kingdoms." Zach was watching the lawyers as he said this.

"Come on, Zach, Yeshua's 'Kingdom of God' is about a world where people love one another and support one another, and where God the Almighty is very close by and really wants us all to become loving people," Ruth said.

Then, someone with a loud voice from the back of the crowd asked whether God, who is far away, knows anything about people.

Yeshua smiled and turned to all in the house, "Every hair of your head is numbered," he replied.

"That's something very different from a God who only sees us from far away," said Joseph.

Next thing, Zach felt a strong nudge. It was from Ruth and she was pointing to the roof.

"Joseph," Zach said as he looked at the roof, "you are going to need a new roof! What will Simon say?"

A group of four men had quietly been removing brushwood and clay off the roof and had made an opening between two of the large beams. Before anyone had noticed, they began lowering a mat.

"There is a man lying on the mat," Ruth whispered.

"He is very thin. And look at his legs! – he is a cripple," Ruth murmured, obviously upset.

The mat landed right beside Yeshua, who smiled. He looked up at the four men on the roof with admiration at their great faith in his ability to cure. Then he turned to the man on the mat and said, "My son, your sins are forgiven."

For Zach, the power of Yeshua's words felt like a boat hitting a rock in the sea. But as he and his pals looked around, all they saw were stony-faced and silent people.

"The lawyers don't seem too happy with Yeshua's remark," Zach suggested.

"I agree," said Joseph. "They even look a bit angry."

Zach heard one of the lawyers complain, "How does he dare talk like this? This is blasphemy! God is the only one who can forgive sins!"

Ruth turned pale and slowly said, "Blasphemy means stoning to death." She moved closer to Zach and held on to his arm.

"Ruth, Yeshua will not be fazed by them," Zach said.

Yeshua heard the complaints and accusations too. He turned to the group of lawyers and quietly but firmly asked them, "Why do you think such things? Is it easier to say to this paralysed man, 'Your sins are forgiven' or to say, 'Get up, pick up your mat, and walk'?"

The lawyers just looked at him, trying to hide their feelings. But Yeshua continued, "I will prove to you, then, that the 'Son of Man' has authority on earth to forgive sins."

"What does 'Son of Man' mean?" Ruth asked in a whisper.

"I have heard Yeshua sometimes call himself that," Stephen replied. "It comes from the prophet Daniel. By using 'Son of Man' Yeshua avoids saying 'me', 'I', 'my' and so on."

"Basically, he doesn't want the focus on himself," Zach added. Ruth nodded.

There was complete silence inside and outside the house, broken only by a few coughs. But Zach decided that this was not the silence of peace which he often felt on the lake. No, it was a silence of expectation, with some aggression, like watching a fight between two strong men. Who would win?

The silence seemed to last an age. But then, as if the time was up and the fight was over, Yeshua turned and, looking with kindness at the man on the mat, said, "I tell you, get up, pick up your mat, and go home!"

Well, there was consternation then. Everyone was shoving and pushing to get a good look at the paralytic. Everyone wanted to see if he would be cured.

Those outside the house were hardly able to see anything but, happily, the gang were there right beside the paralytic.

Then, to their great relief and delight, they saw the young man begin to straighten himself from his crouched position and slowly stand up. He appeared completely healed.

The man stepped towards Yeshua and embraced him. There were tears rolling down his cheeks. Yeshua held him in a strong embrace and then quietly, with a smile, pointed to the front door, and the way home. As the young man made his way through the rejoicing, shouting crowd, he kept saying, "Thank you, Yeshua, thank you. I knew you could heal me." He also knew that he was going home to a completely new life.

Meanwhile, when the gathered crowd outside the windows and doors realised what had happened, their loud cheers joined those of the people inside.

"We have never seen anything like this!" many said.

This joy, however, did not seem to affect the lawyers. They half-smiled, pretending to be happy with the cure, but Zach and his friends knew that they were anything but.

"Why are the lawyers not happy?" Ruth asked.

Stephen said nothing, and watched them leave without a word.

"I think they are furious," Joseph suggested.

"I think you are right, Joseph," Zach agreed, "but the pity is, many of those lawyers are good men who fast and pray and give alms to the poor. I can't understand why they are so upset at the cure of the poor paralytic."

Chapter 6

"How can Yeshua associate with sinners?" Zach asked. "Our teachers tell us that good people should never mix with sinners."

"Maybe our teachers are wrong. Is Matthew not a man like any other? Are we not all sinners?" Stephen asked.

"Of course we are," Zach had to agree, "but we don't fill the pockets of Herod and his gang with poor people's money."

"I think Yeshua is sympathising with Matthew because of the death of his wife and now there is no one at home," Ruth suggested.

"Maybe, who knows? I would love to know what they are talking about," Zach added.

Zach, Stephen and Ruth couldn't believe their eyes when Matthew closed his ledgers, passed them to his secretary, and began walking along with Yeshua. Simon, Andrew, James and John were almost speechless.

"What have we let ourselves in for?" they muttered.

"Actually," Zach suggested, "now that I think of it, tax-collectors have an unpopular job, but it gives them a secure way of life with a good income. So, if Matthew is leaving his job he is making a huge leap of faith in Yeshua and his project."

"You are so right," said Ruth, now looking with admiration at Matthew. "A huge leap of faith."

"Mind you, he couldn't make a huge leap of body," Joseph suggested with a smile. Ruth gave him a dig in the ribs.

"There must be a lot of good in Matthew if Yeshua has chosen him," Ruth added.

Later in the week Matthew held a feast in his house for Yeshua.

It was a lovely Sabbath Day later that month.

"Look at the sea, the jetty — and look at the birds — isn't life great?" Zach asked, having got over the forebodings felt earlier on in the month.

"It is a really beautiful day," Ruth replied, "and we are so lucky to live in such a great place."

The blue sea stretched out before them. All along the shore there were groups of houses and farms. Jutting into the sea was the Zebedee jetty where their fishing boats were anchored. There was no fishing on the Sabbath and so the boats were quietly bobbing up and down, tied to the jetty. A gentle breeze blew. Near the boats, wading in the water, were some of the local birds, two avocets and some stilts, the former with their long legs and long up-curved bills, the latter with their extremely long legs and long, thin, straight bills.

Ahead of the gang, walking and talking together, were Yeshua and 'The Four' along with some others, including some Pharisees.

"I wonder what the Pharisees are doing walking along with Yeshua," Stephen said. Zach and Ruth were still admiring the scenery.

"Zach, Ruth, we had better keep up with the group," Stephen suggested.

Zach, without thinking, was plucking corn. Others were too. The corn was ready for harvesting. The Pharisees, however, on seeing them plucking and eating corn, turned to Yeshua and said, "Look, it is against our law for your disciples to do that on the Sabbath!"

The group had forgotten the strict law that defined plucking corn on the Sabbath as work. Plucking corn was considered the same as reaping and preparing a meal.

"Did you hear that, Zach? I think they want Yeshua to order us to stop eating the corn immediately, and if Yeshua is a holy man, holy as they define it, he has no choice," muttered Stephen.

"The Pharisees look like human avocets with their up-turned bills and beady eyes, hoping to catch their prey," Ruth suggested.

Yeshua replied to the Pharisees, "The Sabbath was made for the good of people; people were not made for the Sabbath. So the 'Son of Man' is Lord, even of the Sabbath."

When the gang heard that they laughed.

"How is it that Yeshua seems to get to the bottom of every issue so easily?" Zach asked. "Of course humans existed before the Sabbath and the

Sabbath is merely there to help us, not to weigh us down. But why didn't our Rabbi or any of us think of that before?"

"It also means that our relationship with God is much more than just observing the Sabbath rules. It's reasonably easy to keep most of the religious rules and regulations – and at the same time to love no one," Stephen added.

"I will have to tell my dad that when he is preparing for the Synagogue meeting next Sabbath that, in Yeshua's view, people are more important than any rituals or books or even sacred objects," Ruth smiled.

CHAPTER 7

It was two weeks later, again on the Sabbath, when the gang next saw Yeshua. It was pouring rain so, instead of preaching outside, he had decided to go into the synagogue.

People were obviously watching out for Yeshua's arrival, while pretending not to. At first the three gang members wondered why this was so, but then they noticed a man in the congregation who had a withered hand. He was sitting over beside the wall.

"That's it," whispered Zach. "The people are afraid that Yeshua will break the Sabbath laws by curing the man, since they know that he will heal the poor and the disabled regardless of the Sabbath law. Yes, that's it!"

"They probably believe that if he does cure the man, the lawyers could charge him and so cause trouble in our town. Nobody wants trouble. And, yes, look at the lawyers." Stephen, as he said this, nodded towards the top seats in the synagogue.

"It's a pity Ruth isn't here to see this," said Zach.

"Who is the one with the fine cloak?" Joseph enquired.

"He is a well-known lawyer from Jerusalem, one of the brightest. I hear he's on the High Priest's Council," an old man near Zach replied. "The Council in Jerusalem is presided over by the High Priest himself."

The three young people then wondered if Yeshua's coming to the synagogue was a good idea at all.

"The authorities in Jerusalem must be beginning to spy on Yeshua," whispered Stephen, his eyes focused on the lawyers in the front seats. "And remember what we learned. If I accidentally cut myself on the Sabbath with a knife, I may bandage the cut but I am not allowed to use ointment that will cure me, that would be doing something on the Sabbath."

Zach shook his head and said, "How will Yeshua face someone with that mind-set sitting there in the front seat?"

Just then, there was a great stir with whispering and shuffling all over the synagogue. Yeshua had arrived at the back door. His very presence had made everyone turn around, including those in the front seats.

"His gentle and caring features light up our synagogue," Stephen said with a smile, as he watched Yeshua come into the synagogue.

"Look, he has seen the man with the withered hand," Joseph observed tapping Stephen. The disabled man had been half-hiding over at the wall.

Yeshua smiled and clearly said to the man with the withered hand, "Come up here to the front."

The man at first didn't want to budge. Yes, he wanted to be healed but not now, not in front of all these people. But, finally, he hesitantly got up, looking rather sheepish, and did as Yeshua asked. Yeshua then turned to those who obviously were not happy with what he might be about to do, especially those in the front seats, and said, "What does our Law allow us to do on the Sabbath? To help or to harm? To save someone's life or to destroy it?"

Most people were reluctant to answer but the man next to Zach said quietly, "You are forbidden to help anyone unless his life is in danger. You know the law. This man's life is not in danger."

"How dare you come here and try to change our lives and our beliefs!" said another man, more loudly. He had a long beard on a protruding chin. His mouth was firmly set in a sneer.

Someone else called out, "Go back to where you came from and leave us alone!"

"Why not keep the law, for God's sake? That's what God asks us to do, no more," an older man joined in. He was close to where the lawyers were seated at the front of the synagogue.

However, the regal-like visitor from Jerusalem, the local Pharisees, and teachers of the Law in the front seats sat quietly with stony faces.

"Their silence is as cold as the eyes of a snake before it bites you," Zach said, louder than he should have.

Yeshua became very upset then and looked quite angrily at the self-important group. No discussion, no hope of discussion!

Joseph thought he heard Yeshua say, "How will I ever get through to them?"

Yeshua turned and looked at the man with the withered hand whose whole demeanour said, 'It's ok, Yeshua! I really do want to be cured but don't cure me now, maybe later after sunset or tomorrow would be better, when the Sabbath will be over.'

With great kindness, Yeshua said to the man with the withered hand, "Stretch out your hand!"

The frail, fearful, poorly-dressed man did as he was told. There was complete silence in the synagogue.

"Look at the lawyers! They are furious... look at them," Zach murmured. "Why are they so annoyed?"

Stephen said, "They are furious that their safe way of life is being threatened."

Meanwhile, the poor man, the centre of the conflict, couldn't believe what was happening. 'Why,' he wondered, 'is Yeshua confronting the whole synagogue on my behalf? Here is someone who seems to think that I, the sinner with the withered hand, am in some way special and even worth having a fight over.'

Tears began to trickle from his eyes and through them he looked down at his hand and saw that it was now entirely normal! He no longer bore the sign of God's anger.

Yeshua stepped forward and hugged him. The man was shaking with emotion, a mixture of disbelief and elation. "Thank you, Yeshua! Thank you, Master!" he whispered. He could hardly talk with the shock.

Well, if Yeshua was angry with the hardness of heart of those in the synagogue, the Pharisees and the man from Jerusalem were even angrier. After the meeting they stormed out of the synagogue. People made way for them. The well-dressed visitor, in particular, stared out the door into some unknown future.

Meanwhile, Ruth was at home lying in her bed, sick. The rest of the gang were anxious to see her. When they arrived at her house she was more than eager to talk to them, even though she wasn't well. But before they could say anything, she blurted out, "Just a few minutes ago, a group of Pharisees and, believe it or not, some of the group who support Herod and his henchmen, were passing down the street outside my window. You know the ones from the big houses up the hill. And what do you think?"

"We have no idea!" they all replied, glad that she was so full of energy.

"Were they talking about Yeshua's cure of the man in the synagogue?" Zach suggested.

"Did Yeshua cure someone?" she asked, but obviously her news was far more urgent.

"Get on with it, Ruth," urged Zach.

"You won't believe it," Ruth continued. "They were obviously angry, and one of them said, 'We will have to get rid of that troublemaker!' Then someone else said 'You mean the sinner from Nazareth?' Then one of them with a high-pitched voice added, 'Of course! The law-breaker and blasphemer!' And then one with a deep voice and a Jerusalem accent slowly said, 'The sooner the better for us all – yes, we will have to kill Yeshua of Nazareth. He is a danger to us all, and possibly even a danger to our nation.'"

"And then they were gone down the street. That is as much as I could make out. At first I didn't know who the people were, since I only heard what they were saying without seeing them, and I didn't recognise any of the voices. But when they passed I got out of bed, even though I am not supposed to, and peeped out the window. I saw some Pharisees and some Herodians. And with them was a man with a very expensive-looking cloak. They were scary people."

When Ruth had finished, the three were stunned.

"Will we tell Yeshua this new twist to the story, Zach?" Stephen asked quietly and slowly. He was trying to think if there were any other way of dealing with the situation.

"Maybe Yeshua already knows," said Zach, smiling and trying to lessen the tension since he realised that Ruth was sick and didn't need any stress. Her face was quite flushed and yet her hands were pale.

"What happened in the synagogue?" she asked anxiously.

In the end, after discussing the whole incident for over an hour, the gang decided that Yeshua had to be told about the rising anger among some of the leaders and teachers of the Law.

That evening, Zach met his brother John and told him the story.

"Zach, Yeshua is aware of the problem. We all are," said John, "but if he doesn't continue he will be telling us that what he has to say is not all that important. As you may be beginning to understand, what Yeshua has to say and do for us is more than important, it is vital for our lives. And, Zach, Yeshua fears no one and, indeed, why should he?"

Chapter 8

"I hear that Yeshua is deciding today," said James, as he neared the base of the hill outside Capernaum.

"He will certainly need some more helpers. His message is so important for us all," replied John.

When they were settled, Yeshua began explaining that the message of the 'kingdom' had to be passed on and he would need a number of helpers to travel with him and work with him.

Then, in a clear voice, Yeshua introduced the names of his future helpers. The first person he introduced was Simon. It was really confirming his earlier call to Simon, but he said to him, "You are Peter."

"Peter? Yeshua is calling your brother Simon a 'rock'," said Zach to Joseph.

"Yes, that is a good name for him," Joseph said with a big smile.

"This 'rock' must be very happy to be chosen as number one. He is a good man. Andrew must be next," Ruth said.

Andrew was next. So, the future helpers included the two sons of Jona.

Yeshua then called James and John, but he also gave them a new name. He called them 'Sons of Thunder'.

"I shouldn't say it, Zach," Stephen said, "but that is a good name for your brothers. Both James and John are physically and mentally very strong, maybe even tough-minded."

"Sometimes, close to ruthless," Zach agreed, "but they are good people all the same, good brothers to have."

Matthew the tax-collector, now firmly one of the group, despite his past, was also confirmed as one of the group of helpers.

"That was expected," Stephen murmured, "but who will be next?"

"It's James bar Alpheus. He has been with the other five for quite some time. He lives only a short distance from our house," Joseph remarked.

James bar Alpheus was stocky and quite tall, with dark hair, very distinctive, intense eyes and a well-trimmed beard.

"He seems self-confident, but then looks can deceive," Zach commented.

"The man beside me just told me that he is related to Yeshua," Ruth said.

"There are certain resemblances all right," Zach agreed.

The next person was called Philip. He was of average height and dressed well. The gang later found out that he came from Bethsaida, the home town of Simon, now Simon Peter.

"He seems to be a gentle person," remarked Ruth.

"Philip means lover of horses," said Stephen.

"It would take you to know that, Stephen," Zach chuckled.

A man named Bartholomew was then asked to join the group.

"Look! Philip is smiling. He and Bartholomew must know each another!" Ruth announced.

"I wonder where Bartholomew comes from?" Stephen asked.

"He comes from Cana," a man beside Stephen replied. "I was at a wedding there and met both Bartholomew and Philip. Yeshua was also at that wedding."

Bartholomew with his red, plump face, perpetual smile and arched, bushy eyebrows that seemed to join in with his laughter, was obviously a happy person.

Yeshua introduced his next choice. He was thin but strong, and had a long face and a very firm, determined mouth.

"I think that's Simon!" Zach said. "He is a Zealot. Some people even call him 'Simon the Zealot'. I heard that Zealots want all the Romans kicked out of our country by whatever means, and the kingdom of Israel firmly established."

"Why would Yeshua want a radical like him as a helper?" Joseph asked, pretending to cut someone's throat with a dagger.

The gang giggled but let it pass. They all felt that Yeshua knew best. But then Stephen had an idea.

"Joseph, your brother Simon is now called Peter so as not to be mixed up with 'Simon the Zealot', whom I presume remains Simon," Stephen suggested.

"You're right!" Joseph smiled.

"Our 'Zealot' must be a very strong-minded person," Ruth added.

"Maybe we are judging him on what we already know," Zach responded.

"I think that his enemies would need to look out," Ruth smiled as she spoke.

The next three chosen were complete strangers to the gang. The first was called Thomas 'The Twin'.

Thomas was quite Roman in his looks, with hazel eyes and a large nose, but he wasn't very strong physically. He seemed fairly tense. It was only in the weeks that followed that the gang found out that he was a most generous person, the kind who would walk two miles with you if you asked him to walk one. On the other hand, he was also someone who was slow to accept anything he was told, unless he was completely convinced that it was true.

The last two introduced were called Thaddeus Jude and Judas. Thaddeus Jude smiled most of the time and seemed to be a happy man.

Judas, on the other hand, didn't seem to laugh much but rather quietly smiled, without much of himself in the smile, at least that's what Ruth felt.

"Zach, Judas seems like a strong character, though I guess that he may suffer from a little impatience. Would you think so?" Ruth asked quietly.

"Yeshua chose him, so he must be a person who can spread 'the kingdom' message," Zach replied.

Zach was to be constantly amazed over the years at the insights of Ruth about people they met. She was nearly always right.

"I heard a few people behind me saying that Judas comes from the town of Keriot," said Stephen. And later they discovered that Judas, like Matthew, was good with money.

When the complete group was finally standing there with Yeshua, they numbered twelve, not including Yeshua.

"To see so many men with different characters and backgrounds is really interesting," said Stephen.

"Well if anyone can make a group work together, it's Yeshua," remarked Joseph.

"It's a great way to secure the future of his teaching in case anything happens to him," Zach added.

"Don't say that, Zach," pleaded Ruth.

"They're back!" cried Ruth.

"Who's back?" Zach asked.

But then the gang saw them. Three well-dressed lawyers had entered the town.

"They look so sure of themselves," Ruth decided.

"I would call it arrogance," Stephen added.

A fairly large crowd was gathering.

"Look at those people! They seem so impressed by these lawyers. That's what worries me," Zach added.

And then it happened. The visitors from Jerusalem pointed at Yeshua and one of them with a loud voice said, "He has Beelzebul in him! It is the chief of the demons who gives him the power to drive them out." It was a small, stocky man who pronounced this loudly. He had a high-pitched, sharp voice. Everyone who had gathered there was able to hear what was said.

Ruth turned to Zach in complete horror.

"Surely that couldn't be true, Zach?" she gasped.

Zach was speechless. Stephen, as often happened, went into himself as he listened and watched in silence. The four members of the gang normally believed what people of education or high rank told them. Soon, some of the crowd began nodding their heads.

The person behind Zach said, "I always thought so. It was too good to be true."

But then, to everyone's amazement, instead of Yeshua going to the visitors from Jerusalem, Yeshua called them... and they went to him, yes, the educated ones from Jerusalem went to Yeshua when he called them.

"How can Satan drive out Satan?" Yeshua firmly asked them. He was looking directly at the three visitors. "If a country divides itself into groups which fight each other," Yeshua spelled it out for them, "that country will fall apart. If a family divides itself into groups which fight each other, that family will fall apart. So if Satan's kingdom divides into groups, it cannot last, but will fall apart and come to an end. No one can break into a strong man's house and take away his belongings unless he first ties up the strong man; then he can plunder his house."

What Yeshua said was so clear and seemed so obvious. What were the visitors going to say now?

"Maybe these lawyers from Jerusalem are wrong," a man behind Ruth murmured. Ruth heard him and smiled.

"Zach," she whispered, "look at our visitors now. They seem quite unsure of themselves."

"You're right!" Zach smiled with delight as he looked at the visitors, "but what did you expect, Ruth?" and then Zach looked at Yeshua.

"Look! Yeshua is not finished with them yet," he said.

"I assure you," continued Yeshua, looking unwaveringly at the three visitors, "that people can be forgiven all their sins and all the evil things they may say. But whoever says evil things against the Holy Spirit will never be forgiven, because he has committed an eternal sin."

Yeshua stopped speaking then and waited to see if the visitors had anything to say. But there was a stony silence. And the visitors took a step away and turned their backs on Yeshua, while they whispered together. Only occasionally did they steal some angry looks at Yeshua over their shoulders.

"There is nothing we can do now," the eldest lawyer murmured, "but we will not let him get away with this."

"They look afraid," said Zach. "They probably are good people in many ways but they shouldn't be trying to oppose Yeshua. They will never outwit or out-argue him. It's quite sad that they are so closed-minded."

"They're leaving!" said Ruth, as she watched the oldest lawyer take a few steps away from where Yeshua stood.

"Like a flock of birds, at one moment our visitors from Jerusalem are trying to find a way to better Yeshua," said Zach with quiet delight. "The next moment they are quickly 'flying away'. There was no apology, just a hasty withdrawal."

"What they said was terrible, Zach. Should they not have apologised?" asked Stephen, still annoyed.

Zach shook his head while Ruth watched the visitors as they disappeared over the hill, on their way to report to their mentors in Jerusalem.

A short time after that, the gang noticed a visitor to their town whom they had never seen before. With her were some other visitors.

"Zach, look at that woman over there. Who is she?" asked Stephen.

"Whoever she is she is very beautiful," replied Zach. "What do you think, Ruth?"

"I agree with you, Zach," she said. Ruth had been watching the woman closely. "She has a constant smile," Ruth continued, "and peace seems to be radiating from her. Her eyes are quite like Yeshua's, dark, intelligent and loving. The way she moves, too, is somehow different. There is no rush, no unnecessary movement. Do you think that she could be Mary, Yeshua's mother? I think Mary is the name of Yeshua's mother."

"That makes sense, Ruth... she is like Yeshua in so many ways," Zach answered.

"I had heard my mother say that Yeshua's mother is beautiful, she met her some years ago... my mother wasn't exaggerating," Stephen added, equally enthralled.

As they looked around they saw that many other people were looking at her.

"Isn't it amazing, that someone could arrive in a town and in no time, without lifting a finger, be the talk of the town?" Joseph finally spoke.

When Mary and some of her extended family had arrived, Yeshua was having a meal in Peter's house with the chosen twelve, now called the 'Apostles' or the 'Twelve', and some local people. But rather than barge into the group, Mary sent in word to Yeshua to say that she and some of the family were outside. The message was quietly passed on to Yeshua.

Yeshua gave a broad smile, then quietly stood up and asked those with whom he was eating, "Who is my mother? Who are my brothers?"

The group didn't know what to say, but then they saw Mary outside the door.

Yeshua smiled again and said, with arms outstretched embracing, as it were, the group at the meal, "Look! Here are my mother and my brothers! Whoever does what God wants is my brother, my sister, and my mother." The seated group applauded Yeshua as he went to his mother and embraced her.

Yeshua's mother stayed for some days and she met all the Twelve and many others who followed Yeshua, including the gang. All agreed and told her, that Yeshua was truly special. Many of them shared stories of what had happened in their lives – the cures, the casting out of demons and the healing of the sick. But soon all who spoke to her realised, even though she never stopped anyone speaking, that she already knew what Yeshua could do and how special he was. Mary did not say much, but her very presence gave all who met her great happiness and peace.

When his mother and his relations had gone Yeshua continued his teaching by the sea and the crowds were again so large that he asked James, as he had done before, to bring a boat around so that he could sit in it and avoid being crushed. When the boat was anchored about twelve metres into the sea, Yeshua began to teach.

As the gang sat there listening to him, they could smell the fresh air, hear the birds, see the sea and the hills, the farms and vineyards, flocks of sheep, herds of goats and cattle.

"I feel so happy and fortunate to be alive," Ruth murmured.

"So do I," said Zach.

That afternoon, Yeshua, with his clear resonant voice, told many stories. There was laughter and fun and at the same time those who listened were growing in understanding. Some of the stories could have had different meanings, but Yeshua allowed the listeners to think about them and over time discover what he meant.

A short time before Yeshua had finished speaking a small group of people arrived and sat near to the gang. It became evident before very long that they were not admirers of Yeshua.

One of them asked in a loud voice, "Our lives are fine the way they are. Why should we change?" His beard was long and his voice was loud but not that clear. Yeshua however, nodded, showing that he understood. Then another of the small group joined in.

"We are followers of Abraham, Moses and Elijah. Why should we need your ideas?" This time it was a lawyer. He continued, "We know and always follow God's law and, as far as we can see, you don't understand God's law at all or grasp its importance."

Having listened carefully to the questions, Yeshua smiled graciously and then quietly pointed to a hill just west of where the crowd was sitting. On the hillside was a farmer looking at his wheat crop. He was walking up and down the pathways between long fields just as he would have done in the planting season. Yeshua turned the whole scene into a story.

"Once there was a man who went out to sow grain. As he scattered the seed in the field, some of it fell on the path, and the birds came and ate it up. Some of it fell on rocky ground, where there was little soil. The seeds soon sprouted, because the soil wasn't deep. Then when the sun came up, it burned the young plants, and because the roots had not grown deep enough, the plants soon dried up. Some of the seed fell among thorn bushes, which grew up and choked the plants, and they didn't bear any grain. But some seed fell on good soil, and the plants sprouted, grew, and bore grain. Some had thirty grains, others sixty, and others one hundred."

"Imagine wheat with a hundred grains!" said Zach, smiling broadly.

That evening, the gang puzzled over the story of sowing the seed for a long time. In the end Yeshua helped them to make sense of it. So, when their families met a few days later for a meal and their parents asked if any of the gang would explain what the story meant, they were ready. Zach agreed to start.

"Well," he began, "the seed is Yeshua's message as to how we can change our lives for the better. Unfortunately, some of us have hardened hearts. We hear Yeshua's teaching alright but are unwilling to accept it and easily fool ourselves into believing that it is not for us, so we don't change."

"We saw that with our visitors from Jerusalem," Ruth added. Zach did not deny or confirm that but smiled at Ruth and continued.

"Secondly, the 'rocky soil' people live on the surface of their lives. They hear Yeshua's teaching but, since they don't really take anything very seriously, they soon give up trying when difficulties arise."

"As for the 'thorn people', they are trapped. We all know, when preparing the fields for planting some farmers merely burn or cut off the tops off the thorn bushes without taking out the roots, so that the thorns grow again and smother the new growth. So, these 'thorn people' find that though they really do listen and decide to change and become better people, their built-in habits of thought and action, which they have been practising daily over many years, get the better of them and smother them. In fact, we asked Yeshua to clarify this for us and he explained that 'The worries about this life, the love of riches, and all other kinds of desires crowd in and choke the message and it doesn't bear fruit.'

"And then there is the last group. These very fortunate people, who having heard Yeshua's message, try to practise it with all their heart, soul and passion, and never give up. These find that life becomes better than they could ever have hoped for, beyond their wildest dreams – that is the hundred-fold crop."

When Zach was finished speaking everyone was extremely impressed.

"Zach is a born teacher," Stephen confided to Zach's mother.

Discussion about what Zach had said went on for a long time and everyone became involved. Later that evening the gang, under pressure, agreed that Ruth could inform the parents of a practice that they, the gang, had taken up.

"Well," said Ruth, looking over at Zach and the others, as if to say she had no choice but to explain, "Zach, Stephen, Joseph and I have begun praying each morning and evening. Yeshua some time ago had brought to our attention Psalm 139 which says,

'O Lord, you have examined me and you know me.
You know everything I do.
From far away you understand all my thoughts.
You see me whether I am working or resting.
You know all my actions.
Even before I speak, you already know what I will say.'

"So, as he has explained before, only very few words are necessary in prayer since God is within us and already knows what we will pray about, so that is how we pray. Also, being allowed to call God our heavenly Father makes all the difference."

"Yeshua told us a story," Stephen explained, "about how change in humans takes place. It goes like this, 'A man scatters seed in his field. He sleeps at night, is up and about during the day, and all the while the seeds are sprouting and growing. Yet he doesn't know how it happens. The soil itself makes the plants grow and bear fruit; first the tender shoot appears, then the head, and finally the head is full of grain. When the grain is ripe, the man starts cutting it with his sickle, because harvest time has come.'"

All at the meal that night were delighted with the gang, with what they had learned and with their growing maturity. They also recognized the immense influence Yeshua was having on them.

CHAPTER 9

"Are we all ready?" John asked.

Salome, John and Zach were preparing for an outing. James was already down at the boats with Yeshua and the rest of the Twelve.

"We're here, Salome," Stephen and his mother Sarah put their head around the door. They had a basket with them and were well dressed for the trip.

Ruth, however, was still at home and would not be with the gang since she had picked up a nasty chill. Zach at first wasn't sure that he would go without her but in the end he agreed to join the others in the boats.

They took off slowly but soon a gentle breeze filled out the sails and they were on their way.

"The joy of sailing is difficult to explain," Zach told Stephen, who was not from a fishing family. "It needs to be experienced at first hand. Each time I set off in one of our boats I feel really happy and excited – the wind in my face, the birds swooping down around the boat, the water quietly slapping at the hull, the sails rustling and putting pressure on the mast, eager to do their job."

As Zach looked back, the shore got farther and farther away. Stephen had brought a flute and started playing some well-known songs. Some of the group were singing along. Others were feeling the water as it slid by.

"Zach, look at the white-tailed eagle," Joseph called. He was in his element.

Zach looked and sure enough there it was, the king of birds. But he also noticed some clouds in the north-east.

"I don't think it's anything much, James, but there are some clouds to the north-east," Zach pointed out quietly, not to alarm anyone.

"John and I have been watching that, I hope we're wrong," James replied.

"What do you mean by that?" asked Zach with a worried look.

"Occasionally, Mount Hermon, Mount Hauran and the Plateaus of Trachonitis see us on the sea and try to get rid of us by blowing us away."

"We're not in any danger, are we?" Zach asked, who until then had not been allowed to go out in weather that was in any way threatening.

But James didn't immediately answer him as he was shouting to Peter in the other boat and pointing to the mountains and the clouds that were now getting bigger. Peter had noticed them as well and looked worried. The wind was getting stronger. And by now both boats were a long way from the shore.

"Zach, sorry for not answering your question," James turned back to Zach. "Take a look at those birds over there. You see the way they are upset? They are telling us that a storm is coming... We must just pray that it isn't too bad."

"Should we turn back?" Zach asked.

"Take a look. We are miles from shore."

James and John, and Peter and Bartholomew in the other boat, began pulling down the sails.

"We'll be all right. James and John know what to do," Salome comforted Sarah, although she was actually quite worried, "Zach, keep away from the sides."

"Mum, I'll be all right. Dad, James, John and I are used to squalls like this." But it was more bravado and a petty annoyance at being treated as if he were still a child that made Zach pretend to be sure of himself.

His mother on the other hand, though she had a smile of sorts, was obviously not used to this type of storm. In truth, none of the fishermen in either boat were.

Then it happened. A large wave came over the side of James' boat and drenched everyone. And then that was followed by another and another. John, shouting over the wind, asked everyone to quickly use the bailers and bail out the rising water at their feet.

"Zach, there's more coming in than we're able to cope with!" Stephen said.

Zach looked over at Peter's boat and they were faring no better.

"Are we in danger, James?" Zach shouted.

"Pray to God, Zach," exhorted John, who was beside James. "We are in great danger!"

Stephen, now very pale, began to vomit. His mother Sarah quickly moved over beside him. Zach was getting extremely tired bailing out water as it steadily rose in the boat. Everyone was soaked.

Then another huge wave hit James' boat. Everyone was thrown forward. Two of them fell down but were only bruised. "That felt like being hit by a huge rock!" Stephen, now half-recovered, shouted over what had become a whistling gale. The boat seemed to just stop in the water. Zach was sure that the boat was about to break up, but it took the blow and remained in one piece. It was only when James became frantic that Zach started believing that the lives of everyone in the boats were over.

'How will my dad cope without his wife and three sons?' Zach asked himself. For some reason he looked over at Yeshua to see how he was taking it. It was difficult to see him since the waves were so high and the spray was everywhere, but then Zach spotted him.

"Stephen," he shouted over the howling winds, "Yeshua is asleep at the back of Peter's boat!" Stephen, still looking very sickly, looked over at Yeshua in disbelief.

Then another huge wave hit the boats. Peter's boat got a terrible battering. He was terrified. It was Yeshua who had suggested that they go out to sea in the first place. He started shouting at Yeshua.

"Teacher, don't you care that we are about to die?" he roared.

At the sound of Peter's voice, Yeshua's eyes opened and, after taking a quick look around, he stood up. With his left hand he held on to the ropes that came down from the mast, and then, as the spray covered him he lifted up his right hand and said to the wind, "Be quiet!" Yeshua was like a father giving out to his child for misbehaving.

And then looking at the mountainous waves he said, "Be still!"

Zach couldn't believe what he was hearing. He turned to Stephen.

"Stephen, what is Yeshua doing? Is he gone mad?" Zach asked, his eyes almost popping out of his head.

Stephen looked at Yeshua and with a gentle smile said nothing. Zach couldn't understand Stephen's reaction at all.

However, to Zach's and everyone else's utter shock the wind just stopped obediently and became a mild, respectful breeze again. The huge waves too, removing their white caps, just gave a kind of bow and then disappeared. They were swallowed up and seemed to leave the lake through some hidden door. Only gentle ripples remained and in minutes the clouds were replaced by brilliant sunshine.

Well, what could anyone say? There was complete silence on both boats. No doubt everyone wanted to shout with joy but in the end, having made a few remarks to one another, they just sat down shaking their heads in total disbelief.

"Who is this man," Zach asked Stephen, "that even the winds and the waves obey him?"

"I have never been so scared in my life," Stephen admitted, "but when I saw Yeshua becoming involved I knew we would be safe."

Although Stephen, Joseph and Zach pretended not to notice, the two mothers had their hands up to their faces and were quietly wiping away tears.

On the other boat, Peter, who was mortified at losing his temper, apologised for his outburst to Yeshua. Yeshua gently smiled as if to say 'It's nothing.'

The piece of land where the boats were headed for was now only a short distance away so the sails were raised again.

Soon, carried along by a light breeze from behind, the picnickers reached land in the country of the Ger'asenes. It was a lovely late-afternoon. But the shocks of the day weren't over yet.

When the boats were tied up, and everyone finally stood on firm ground, they all began sharing how they had felt in the midst of the storm.

Zach, for some reason, turned and, to his horror, there was a stark naked man, with ragged hair and a dirty long beard, running towards them, shouting.

"He is heading for Yeshua," Stephen whispered, hoping not to draw the man in his direction.

As the naked man came nearer, everyone could see that he had many scars on his body and nasty red marks around his wrists and ankles. He looked angry and his jaw was clenched in a scowl. At first Peter, James and John thought he might strike Yeshua, who was calmly standing there a little in front of them, and they thought they should do something. But the man quickly flung himself at Yeshua's feet and, with a voice that sounded like a hull scraping against a rock, snarled, "Yeshua, Son of the Most High God! What do you want with me? For God's sake, I beg you, don't punish me!"

"What is your name?" Yeshua asked, looking at the man with full attention.

"My name is 'Legion', there are so many of us," he replied. His eyes were red and one of his ears had a piece missing.

"Us?" whispered Stephen, as the three members of the gang watched in horror. They realised that Yeshua was dealing with many demons. "A Roman legion has six thousand men," Stephen informed them.

"Send us to the pigs, and let us go into them," the man said holding out his hands pleading.

Not far from where the group had landed there was a very large herd of pigs with two herdsmen. Both Zach and Stephen had noticed them when they landed but had paid no attention to them.

Yeshua looked at the man and then nodded as if giving permission. At that the man let out a horrible screech. Almost instantaneously there was a chorus of screeches coming from the herd of pigs, at which point they began to run headlong into the sea. The herdsmen, realising what was happening, ran away.

"The pigs will all be drowned," Stephen said.

Joseph and Zach just stared at the pigs flailing in the water. After a few seconds all of them had disappeared as if they had never existed. Only some white foam remained.

"Did you see that?" Joseph asked. "What now?"

They looked back at the naked man and Yeshua was helping him to his feet. The man looked as if he had no idea what had happened. Salome and Sarah gave him some clothes that had been brought in case they were needed. It was only then that the man realised he was naked. He gratefully took the clothes, washed himself in the sea, and got dressed.

Gone was the aggression, and gone was the terrible stare and the harsh voice. He sat down with the group now arranging the belated picnic, and with obvious thankfulness ate some of the food that had been brought for the trip.

"What will happen to the poor herdsmen?" Zach asked, still not over the disappearance of the pigs.

"I don't blame them for running away as quickly as they did," Stephen replied. But just then the herdsmen and some other people appeared. They walked up to Yeshua who was standing with John and Peter.

"Our men have told us that our pigs ran into the sea," a short, middle-aged man with an angry red face said, addressing Yeshua and John. "I believe that you, Sir," speaking directly to Yeshua, "must have had something to do with it, but we don't understand how or why. And now, Sir, we would like you to leave this area immediately."

"Did you hear that? Aren't they rather foolish asking Yeshua to leave?" Joseph asked, turning to his two companions. "If only they knew what type of man Yeshua is, and how he could change their lives for the better."

"If they had really known Yeshua they would have begged him to stay," Stephen said repeating what Joseph said.

Soon everyone was packing up and making their way to the boats for the return journey. As they were boarding, the man who had been possessed by demons went over to Yeshua and begged him to let him be part of the group, but Yeshua gently said to him, "Go back home to your family and tell them how much the Lord has done for you and how kind he has been to you."

Turning to his two pals Zach remarked, "It is only now that the man realises that he is fully freed of the demons, that his life is normal again and that he has a family and a home and can return to them."

"His sins must have been forgiven," Stephen announced, reflecting on Yeshua's other cures.

"And if he is no longer a sinner then he can return to the Synagogue... look at him now," Joseph added.

With tears streaming down his face, the man embraced Yeshua. He stayed in Yeshua's arms for some time, sobbing and shaking his head. Then one of the women came forward and gave him a lantern.

It was only much later, when James had returned from one of his visits to local towns with Yeshua, that he told Zach, "Remember the man in the country of the Ger'asenes who was possessed of all those demons? I found out a few days ago that he has been going through the cities of the Decapolis, the ten cities, telling everyone about Yeshua and what God has done through him."

"So he has become a follower of Yeshua after all?" replied Zach, delighted with the news.

"Indeed he has," said James.

CHAPTER 10

When the boats finally got back to Capernaum, it was early morning.

"Look, Zach, Ruth's dad is on the jetty," Stephen said very softly. "Something is wrong."

"Could something have happened to Ruth?" Joseph asked, looking at Zach who was staring at Ruth's dad, trying to work out why he would have come to the jetty in the early morning.

"It's probably something to do with the synagogue," said Stephen, realising that Zach was imagining something terrible.

Ruth's dad, Jairus, normally a very happy man, full of life and fun like Ruth, threw himself down in front of Yeshua, as soon as he got out of the boat.

"My daughter is very sick!" Jairus said with tears in his eyes. "Please come and place your hands on her, so that she will get well, and live."

"It *is* about Ruth," Zach mumbled. "She didn't come on the boat trip, but she only had a chill!" His voice rose anxiously, "I shouldn't have gone!"

"Come on," Stephen said, putting his arm around Zach. "How were we to know that Ruth was going to become very ill? Anyway, Yeshua will just go and cure her. Everything will be fine."

"We know that for sure," said Joseph, forcing a smile.

But Zach knew in his bones that Jairus would hardly have come at this hour of the morning unless Ruth's condition was very serious. In fact, to come to Yeshua at all, when Jairus hadn't fully accepted the healings on the Sabbath, did suggest that all other means of curing Ruth had been tried already or had been ruled out.

"Let me come with you, Jairus," Yeshua said, as they quickly walked away from the jetty.

Needless to say, a crowd had gathered, and they, along with the two boatloads, followed Yeshua. As happened before, Yeshua was not very far from being crushed by the crowd around him. Peter, James and John surrounded him and tried to keep him from being trampled.

"Look at all the people pushing and shoving and trying to touch Yeshua. I hope they don't delay him," Zach said.

Then, all of a sudden, Yeshua stopped and said in a strong voice. "Who touched my clothes?"

"What a question!" Stephen exclaimed. "The answer surely is at least fifty people, if not more."

Peter, James and John were also amazed at Yeshua's remark and James asked him, "You see how the people are crowding you. Why do you ask who touched you?"

But Yeshua kept looking around. Then a woman, who appeared to be terrified and was trembling all over, came forward and threw herself at Yeshua's feet.

"What is she doing, Stephen?" Zach asked in desperation.

"Whatever it is, she is very brave to kneel there with that crowd all around her," replied Stephen.

The woman was elderly, and obviously had been suffering a great deal. It showed in her face. Her eyes were tired, with bags underneath them. But she was a striking woman. Between breaths, she told Yeshua, "I've been ill for twelve years and have spent all my money looking for a cure from various doctors but they were no good. I am as bad as ever, if not worse. But I said to myself, 'If I just touch your clothes I will get well.'"

"My daughter," said Yeshua quietly, "your faith has made you well. Go in peace and be healed of your trouble."

At first she was shocked and speechless, but when Yeshua lifted her up from where she was kneeling, she began crying. Yeshua, then, as he often did, gently gave her a hug and sent her on her way. The crowd cheered, realising she had been cured.

"Look, Zach, she is healed! I told you Yeshua can cure Ruth of whatever the problem is." Stephen said, completely sure of this. Zach was still very worried. Joseph was quite convinced that there would be no problem and was still looking at the woman being congratulated after her cure.

"A man is running towards Jairus," Zach suddenly said in a loud voice, and began moving nearer to Yeshua and Jairus. "Let's see if we can hear what the man has to say."

They got closer to Yeshua, elbowing their way past three or four people who were in the way. When the man got to Jairus he spoke very quietly. "Your daughter has died. You don't need to bother the Teacher any longer," he said.

Zach froze. He thought he heard what the man said and hoped he was wrong. "Did you hear that?" he said with tears welling up in his eyes. He stared at Stephen and Joseph looking totally lost.

Stephen and Joseph both put their arms around Zach and they too were crying, "Yes, we heard what he said."

"If Ruth has died, it is more than disastrous," Zach mumbled. "Her thirteenth birthday is in a few weeks and I've organised a special gift for her. Am I not right? This proves once again that God doesn't care about us, as I had always thought."

Meanwhile, Yeshua gently looked at Jairus, who was now in tears, not knowing what to do or where to turn. He, no doubt, even more than Zach and his friends, wondered if he could cope with his daughter's death and knew that his wife and the rest of their family would never be the same again.

"Don't be afraid, only believe," Yeshua said. "Only Peter, James and John are to come with me," he added.

The crowd stopped, knowing that things were not good in Jairus' house, although they hadn't heard the messenger who had spoken to Jairus.

"The girl must be very ill indeed, or worse," one woman said.

"The girl must have died," another bystander guessed.

But then the word was out that she had died and they all wondered if Yeshua could do much now.

"Maybe he could console the family and bless them," one person suggested.

"If only the girl's family had come earlier to Yeshua, he would have been able to do something," someone else said.

"But wasn't Jairus one of the ones who was not too keen on Yeshua and his teaching in the Synagogue, at least in the beginning?" asked another.

Then Joseph, who had separated himself from the crowd, called Zach and Stephen over. He was standing outside a small shop.

"We can take the back way to Ruth's house," Joseph said.

"We are not allowed to follow," Zach and Stephen answered.

"We're not following, we are visiting the house, but not as part of Yeshua's group," Joseph explained. Zach and Stephen were delighted with Joseph's reasoning.

Soon the three were running down a pathway that would lead them to the back of Jairus' house. As they came close, they heard loud weeping and wailing.

"Listen to that, it's true," Zach muttered, as tears again began to pour down his face. Zach couldn't take it in. He was now very angry with God.

There was quite a crowd in the house. The three assumed that Ruth would be laid out in the bedroom beside the kitchen area, which was her space. Quietly they edged up to the window to take a look inside, Zach being first. There Ruth was, pale and still, lying on the bed at the other side of the room. When he saw her he curled up and cried bitterly. The two others then took a look and soon all three were in floods of tears.

"Why all this confusion? Why are you crying? The child is not dead – she is only sleeping!" It was Yeshua speaking in the outer room.

"It's Yeshua," said Stephen.

And then they heard jeering from the people near Yeshua. All three were angry at such disrespect. "What stupid people!" Stephen announced.

But the laughter stopped quickly as Yeshua sternly ordered them all to leave the house. Then the three heard Yeshua and some others enter the room where Ruth lay.

It was now Joseph who peeped through the window and gave a whispered commentary on what was happening.

"Yeshua is moving over to the bed... He seems upset... He is looking at the parents and now at the body of Ruth..."

"Little girl, I tell you to get up," said Yeshua gently.

Joseph motioned his friends to be completely silent. "Did you hear that?"

The three peeped through the window to see if what they hoped would happen, did happen.

"Ruth has opened her eyes!" Stephen whispered as his two friends beside him looked on, speechless.

Zach had to use all his self-control not to shout out, or bang the wall in relief. The tears this time were of happiness.

Ruth, meanwhile, looked around at the people in her room and then slowly got up from the bed and put her arms around Yeshua, who embraced her gently. Then she walked over to her parents and clung on to them. She obviously didn't understand what was happening and wondered why all the people were in her room. Her father and mother were lost for words. Yeshua quietly asked all those in the room to tell no one what had happened. Then he smiled and suggested that maybe Ruth might need something to eat.

But Ruth's mother went immediately to Yeshua and hugged him, weeping. "I should have believed my husband when he explained that you could make all things right for Ruth," she cried.

Outside the window, the pals were laughing and crying with happiness at the same time.

CHAPTER 11

Two months after Ruth's recovery, Yeshua decided to return to Nazareth to visit his mother and extended family. The Twelve, some disciples and the gang went with him, including Ruth who was back in great form. Nazareth was only a few miles away, although it was necessary to climb up into the hills to get there.

"Zach, have you often been to Nazareth?" asked Joseph as they walked relentlessly up the hill towards the town.

"A few times, but before we get there, let's climb up further, over the town. There's a wonderful view from there," Zach suggested.

The group looked at him to see if he were serious, but he was. It was quite an effort and the three young men of the gang were delighted that Ruth had no problem with the extra climb. Indeed she seemed very fit. After a while they reached the top of the mountain.

"What a view!" said Stephen. "I have never before seen the Great Plains from such a height. Seeing this makes the battles of our ancestors so real – so many battles, so many killed... Zach, does that road go the whole way to Egypt?"

"Yes, so John says. And over there you can see Mount Carmel, where Elijah fought the prophets of Baal. And do you see the blue-green line after that? There? That is the Mediterranean Sea."

"It's massive!" said Joseph. "I'd love to go to Tyre and Sidon. My brother told me all about those cities and the huge boats that are there – are we looking towards the West?"

"Yes, the sun goes down near Mount Carmel every evening," Zach replied, pointing to the mountain peak on the horizon.

Ruth smiled as she looked into the distance. "What is that road over there with the camel train on it, Zach?" she asked.

"That is the 'Way of the Sea', the road connecting Damascus with all the sea ports, including Tyre and Sidon," explained Zach.

"Is that Sepphoris just across those hills?" asked Stephen. "It seems immense."

"Yes it is — built by Herod with our exorbitant taxes. But look far away to the north-east, that great snow-covered mountain is Mount Hermon — over here to the east is Mount Tabor. And of course, just ahead of us going south is the road to Jerusalem."

They then began descending the other side of the hill, and there in front of them was Nazareth.

"So this is Yeshua's town. It looks like a lovely place, tucked away in the valley and surrounded by those hills. Look! Nearly all the houses seem to be built of limestone," Ruth said, enthralled by the whole scene.

"I hear the people in Nazareth are very pious, revering the Torah above everything," Stephen remarked.

The following day was the Sabbath, and having spent the previous evening with relations and with Yeshua and his mother, the gang were expecting great things.

As they were about to enter the synagogue, Ruth whispered, "Zach, I have a feeling that Yeshua's views are not popular here. I'll see you after the celebration." She then disappeared with the women into their section behind the partition.

Yeshua had been appointed that day to speak to everyone in the synagogue. The three boys were delighted with his words but, as they looked around, they saw that not everyone shared their excitement.

"Do you feel that there is a certain antagonism here?" Stephen whispered.

A man beside them asked, "Where does this man get his ideas?" It was said in a nasty tone. "What wisdom is this?" was the cynical remark from another man nearby, and he added, "How does he perform miracles?"

Stephen was furious. "I suppose he is referring to Beelzebul or some other Evil One? Those visitors from Jerusalem have caused terrible trouble!"

"Isn't he the craftsman, the son of Mary, and brother of James, Joseph, Judas and Simon? Aren't his sisters living here?" inquired another local person.

"Are they saying that Yeshua is incapable of achieving anything beyond his workman's status?" Stephen murmured, enraged.

"Shouldn't he be called Yeshua bar Joseph, as is traditional?" Zach added.

"Maybe they call him son of Mary because Mary's husband Joseph died many years ago," Joseph said, taking a positive view.

"It seems as if people are blind to Yeshua's achievements. You can see it in their body language and their looks. And they're definitely muttering nasty remarks," Stephen fumed.

"I agree, Stephen," Zach whispered, as he looked around the synagogue.

"I don't like saying it but so do I," said Joseph as he copied the look and posture of a man near them.

Yeshua spoke again.

"Prophets are respected everywhere except in their own hometown and by their relatives and their family," he said.

Except for his mother of course, the gang agreed that it certainly seemed to be true of the people of Nazareth.

Chapter 12

The gang stood outside Peter's house watching the Twelve setting out, two by two, to visit the towns of Galilee, on their first 'missionary journey' without Yeshua. Yeshua stood there, as they left, encouraging them. They carried very little with them – no food, or money, or spare sandals – only walking sticks.

"I am sure that they're all very apprehensive," Zach commented.

"At the same time they appear confident," said Stephen. "Frankly, I am half-envious of them. I would love to be one of them. I hope when I am old enough that I will be chosen to join them."

"You would be great," Ruth affirmed.

"I agree," said Joseph.

"We all do," Zach said, smiling encouragingly at Stephen.

Stephen's face became a little red. His remark had really been merely thinking aloud.

"You're most welcome, Joanna," Zach's mother said, as she stood at her front door.

"And blessings on you, Salome," Joanna replied.

Joanna was a small woman with a big heart and a huge smile. She was the wife of Chuza who worked for Herod at the palace of Machaerus.

"And here's a skin of the best wine from Herod's cellar for you, Salome." Joanna had a mischievous grin on her face as she said this.

"You shouldn't, Joanna," said Salome shaking her head, but delighted at the gift all the same.

"Come on in, what are we standing here for?" Salome said putting her arm around Joanna.

They sat down together, sharing bits of news and catching up on old times. "How is everything at Machaerus, Joanna? I suppose Chuza is extremely busy as usual," Salome asked.

Joanna smiled. "All is well, thank God, but my husband is working too hard. Herodias is throwing a birthday party for Herod Antipas and the preparations are just too much. As far as Chuza can see, everyone from the religious, political, army and secular elite will be there. It will be a 'Who's Who' of Judea and Galilee. Indeed, some may be coming from farther afield. The Roman Governor may even be attending... though I doubt it. He enjoys Caesarea too much."

"I suppose you know that my Zebedee got a call to supply a huge consignment of fish for the occasion?" Salome revealed.

"Yes. Chuza told the chief organizing committee that your husband was very reliable, and he is. So they took my husband's advice... but there is more, Salome. A number of the servants are sick at the moment and they are twenty short in the Palace. I have found sixteen replacements to take their places but I wonder if Zach could organize a few of his friends? My husband would train them in very quickly. It is only for the feast of course."

"I am sure Zach would be delighted, particularly because his brothers are away. Zebedee is also busy going back and forth to Magdala preparing the fish, and Yeshua is away too. Could a girl of thirteen also join them?" Salome added.

"Yes, indeed. There are a good number of girls serving in the court and my husband will keep a good eye on her."

"I think Zach and his pals, Stephen and Joseph, will do that," Salome chuckled. "They guard her like lions."

The gang agreed to go to Machaerus to replace the four sick waiting staff. However, it was agreed that they would be accompanied by Zach's parents and because of this their families were delighted for them. They would be paid handsomely – and have a holiday at the same time. Little did they know!

The journey to Machaerus was a hard five-day trek but it didn't seem so difficult since they saw the beautiful River Jordan valley and the towns on their way. On leaving the river Jordan, they turned to the left and went along the shore of Lake Asphaltites. At Callirrhoe they began the steep climb to Machaerus.

"Look at the walls! They're really thick," Joseph remarked with awe.

"Welcome to Machaerus!" a small, very smartly-dressed, rather rotund man with a happy face, standing at the gate, announced. "My name is Levi, I have been asked to meet you by the Manager of the King's Household. Unfortunately, he is at a meeting with the King at this moment, but let me bring you to his house."

The group went in through large iron gates and turned left.

"Look, Zach!" Stephen whispered. "They are the same soldiers that took John the Baptist away."

"I like their uniform but not the way they treat people," Zach replied very quietly.

"Oh look! Here she is," announced Ruth, as Joanna rounded the corner.

"Sorry for being late. I mistook the time. Life in the past few days has been hectic," Joanna said, opening her arms to them all.

They set off and having passed a number of houses, arrived at Joanna's home.

"Look, the house has two guards at the gate," Joseph murmured.

"What a wonderful house you have, Joanna," Salome said. "I see that it looks out towards the Mediterranean Sea, far in the distance. It's beautiful."

"Yes. Chuza chose this site for us and had the house built to his own specifications," Joanna said proudly.

"And what a lovely quadrangle and fountain – I would say that the three boys would like to sleep here, near the fountain, in their tent," Salome suggested, knowing that the boys loved sleeping in the open.

"But there is plenty of room inside," replied Joanna with a happy shrug.

"Ruth will sleep inside, but the three young 'pilgrims' would enjoy it here," Salome said.

"Great, then, we'll arrange it like that. Is that okay with you, young men?"

"We'd love to camp out here," Zach told her, while the others nodded agreement.

"It's time for something to eat," said Joanna, turning and going into a very large room where there was a table full of all sorts of dishes filled with delicious food. The gang couldn't believe the size of the banquet.

CHAPTER 13

The following morning, the gang were shown how to serve at the feast.

"Do you understand? One more thing, you serve and pour from the right of the guest, slowly... like this." The manager showed them exactly what to do. "Are we clear then?"

The group of twenty all nodded, "Yes, Sir."

"The meal should last for up to five hours. Are you able for that?"

"I think we are," the group answered, amazed at the length of the meal.

"Now, Zach," said the manager, "you will be standing at this table behind one of the dignitaries from Jerusalem. Stephen you can stand beside Zach to his left. You, Joseph... it is Joseph, isn't it?"

"Yes Sir," replied Joseph.

"You can stand over here, three places away from Stephen. You, Ruth, can stand on the other side of Zach... one place to his right, and you Ruth will be serving a Senator from Rome." The manager smiled at her, but in the smile there was a hint of 'I don't expect you to make any mistakes – be careful.'

Zach turned to Ruth and offered quietly, "Anytime you need a rest just give me a nod and I will cover for you."

"Thanks, Zach," she whispered back.

Having shown everyone their places, the manager asked, "Are there any questions?"

"Sir," asked Joseph, "are those goblets made of real gold?"

"Yes, Joseph... and if anyone steals a goblet – if you take a look, they have the King's mark on them — that person may not see the light of day again."

Zach was about to say 'like John the Baptist' but thought the better of it.

"I will leave you now to look around. But go to the kitchens for the first course immediately the gong is struck three times."

When the gang finally got into the kitchens to collect the first course, they couldn't believe the level of tension and activity there. Hundreds of servers were all lined up in different queues to collect the plates. Each plate had a gold rim and was full of delicious fruit.

"You're next in line, Ruth," Zach pointed to the man giving out the plates.

"Ruth, I'll follow you right away," Zach turned to collect the plate he had to carry to the dining hall. In no time they were waiting just outside the hall for the guests to come and sit down.

A huge gong was struck, and it resounded throughout the whole palace. The banquet hall began to fill up.

Zach bent over to Ruth and whispered, "These are the rich and famous of Israel and beyond."

"It's unbelievable!" Ruth whispered back.

Then in came musicians, dancers and acrobats. Joseph pretended to dance and Ruth had to stifle a laugh.

When the musicians, dancers and acrobats came in there was a great feeling of excitement. They had their bodies painted with all sorts of designs and wore clothing different from anything the gang had seen before, full of colours and with beads of all sizes and shapes. They also wore various types of head-dress. Some wore multi-coloured feathers. Many had very short, dark and curly hair. One of them was quite bald with a smile painted around his mouth. The gang were enthralled.

Just then, when all the guests were in their places, King Herod Antipas and his wife Herodias entered the dining hall. There were eight trumpeters playing as they entered. The King was dressed in a fabulous red robe made of silk. He had a gold pendant around his neck, loads of rings on his fingers and a beautiful gold bracelet around each wrist. He also had a crown on his head with numerous jewels in it.

His wife was walking beside him and looked very regal, but she somehow seemed as cold as ice. She was dressed in both black and red silk, with a sparkling diamond-studded gold chain around her neck, and she wore gorgeous pearl bracelets around her wrists. Her dress was covered with exotic ornaments, while on top of her head was a small crown, and it was covered with diamonds, pearls and rubies. She wore stunning shoes, also studded with diamonds. She smiled alright, but her smile was like that of a lioness before she devours you.

When they entered, all the guests stood and clapped and then, after the king sat down, so did everybody else. From that moment on, for over four hours, the gang were kept busy.

The amount of food that the guests ate could have fed the whole population around the Sea of Galilee, with plenty to spare. The amount of wine that was drunk could have filled a few cisterns. And, as the evening went on, the noise of voices in the banquet hall grew louder and louder and some of the musicians could hardly be heard.

About four hours after it all began, the noise suddenly stopped when Herodias' daughter, Shlomit, stepped out onto the floor. Well, she was a sight to see! She had exquisite clothes, but they were quite revealing. First, she faced towards the top table where Herod sat, and bowed in recognition of his status. Then she began to dance.

She was accompanied by a whole group of players and the audience couldn't take their eyes off her. Her dancing began slowly but then she moved faster and faster, forming rings with a kind of silk scarf that she held in her left hand. Then she threw away the scarf and slowed down again. It was obvious that she was becoming more daring, more alluring. Herod was delighted and encouraged her. When she had finished, she bowed to him again, touching the ground with her head, and then slowly straightened up. Somehow, she had the scarf back in her hand and she made a large circle in the air as part of her curtsey.

Herod, absolutely delighted with the performance, swore to his step-daughter, "Ask me for whatever you wish and I will give it to you."

Gazing at her he repeated, "I swear that I will give you anything you ask me for," adding "even as much as half my kingdom!"

"Herod is obviously quite drunk," whispered Zach to Ruth.

"To tell Shlomit that she can have half of his kingdom means that she can become his wife. Herodias won't like that," she replied.

"You're right, Ruth, take a look at Herodias. Her smile is like the snow of Mount Hermon," said Zach.

"She reminds me of a scorpion about to strike," Ruth shuddered.

"Look! Her daughter is going over to her. I hope it's not to ask whether she can become Herod's wife too," Zach grinned. "I'd love to know what they are saying." But his amusement didn't last long. "Ruth, I think I heard Herodias say something about John the Baptist. How do you think he would fit in at this party?"

"You must be wrong. I am sure they don't want the guests to know that John is their prisoner," Ruth whispered. Then she moved forward three steps and smilingly filled the goblet of 'her' Senator from Rome.

"Zach, she is going over to Herod with some request. Maybe she will dance again."

"I can't believe what I just heard!" Zach said, staring aghast at Herod.

"What did she say?" asked Ruth, but Zach had moved over to Stephen who was standing about fifteen feet away.

At that moment Herod called over a soldier, who was standing at one of the entrances to the hall. Herod was furious. There was a kind of madness in his eyes. He murmured something to the soldier who hurried off.

Stephen, Zach and Joseph looked very perturbed, and looked over at Ruth. 'What can they be saying about me?' she asked herself.

Two of the visitors called out for more wine and Stephen and Joseph had to move quickly to fill their glasses. When Joseph had finished pouring he had to fetch more from the cellar. Stephen still had enough wine, but the supervisor was not impressed with their behaviour and spoke sternly to both of them.

Then it happened. The soldier was back. Zach looked over and nearly fainted. There were various stifled screams of disbelief in the dining hall. The soldier was carrying John the Baptist's head, cut off at the neck, on a plate.

"Ruth, it's time for you to leave," said Zach, huge tension on his face.

Ruth couldn't understand what was happening. When she was about to say something Joseph arrived by her side. She hadn't yet seen what the soldier was carrying. Then Chuza, with a deep frown on his face, unexpectedly appeared, just in time to distract Ruth further. The gang swiftly left the dining hall.

"What happened?" asked Ruth, completely confused. "You are all looking so pale."

Zach began to vomit. Stephen was crying and Joseph had a look of terror on his face.

"Let's get you back to the house," said Chuza. Then calling a supervisor he said, "Over here, Rahab, please accompany these young, people to my home at once." Then, turning to Zach and the others, he said, "I am deeply sorry about what has happened. Tell your parents and my wife that I will be home in an hour or so. Now go quickly."

As they left the building with Rahab, Chuza was ordering a servant, "Clean the floor immediately." Then he returned to the dining hall.

An hour and a half later he arrived back to his house. Everyone was still up. Ruth had heard what had happened and she had thanked Zach and the others for keeping her from seeing the Baptist's severed head presented on a plate to Herodias.

"What a terrible evening," said Chuza as he arrived. "Life will be very, very difficult in Machaerus for the foreseeable future. You know the Herods have a mad streak in them. I hope this isn't the beginning of something worse. His father, Herod the Great, as you know, went completely mad towards the end of his life. However, I won't go into that. I recommend a little wine to help us sleep tonight. I normally don't drink but I feel we should have something this evening. And yes, as you probably guessed, it was Herodias who demanded John's head, through her daughter. Her daughter dutifully brought John's head to her mother. But Herod refused to touch it."

"Herodias is obviously truly wicked," Zebedee said quietly.

"Her daughter is probably as bad, if not worse, only younger," replied Chuza.

"Time for bed," said Salome to the gang.

As the three boys went to their tent in the quadrangle, Stephen asked Zach, "Do you think you will ever forget this visit to Machaerus?"

"No, Stephen, how could any of us ever forget such a violent, mindless killing?" Zach replied, with a very dark, angry look. "But it is done now and we have to get on with our lives as best we can."

"You're right... but I never thought I would see such a horrible thing," Stephen added.

"Neither did I," said Joseph who, unusually, was very quiet.

CHAPTER 14

Three months passed. One morning Joseph came to see Zach.

"Did you know that Stephen is away with his dad for a few days?" asked Joseph.

"Yes, it's some research project, I think," replied Zach.

He was about to say more when he noticed the Twelve coming down the road towards the house. "Here comes Yeshua with the Twelve."

As the Twelve came nearer, Yeshua stopped and turning to them said, "Let us go off by ourselves to some place where we will be alone and you can rest a while."

"They certainly need the break," remarked Joseph pretending to fall asleep.

After a few moments of discussion the Twelve seemed happy with Yeshua's idea of taking time out for a rest. Their missionary work had been far more exhausting than they had ever imagined it would be.

"They are going to a quiet place," Zach added. "I hope nobody finds out where or they will be followed." And then he remembered that he had some news.

"Joseph," he said, "Ruth came to our house very early this morning and told us that her family is going to visit some of their extended family in Sepphoris because one of them is ill. She expects to be back in around two weeks."

"She's taking a rest, too?" Joseph said, and then he smiled, "I hope she has a great time. She deserves it. So with Stephen gone to Jerusalem with his dad and Ruth in Sepphoris, I suppose we will have to catch a load of fish and have a feast ready for them when they return."

"What a great idea," Zach agreed.

Then Joseph turned to him, "You know, Zach, Yeshua and the Twelve have a very hard life. I'm so glad they're taking time off. Most people in our town would be dead if they worked as hard as Yeshua." Joseph was looking at the Twelve as he spoke.

Then John caught Zach's eye and, having spoken to Peter and Yeshua, he came up to the two of them and said, "Would you two like to come with us for a short break? Since both of you are good boatmen and physically strong we could do with your help."

Zach looked at Joseph who nodded, evidently delighted to be asked.

"We would love to come!" Zach told John, who explained that they would be setting off shortly. "Great!" said Zach excitedly. "We'll give a hand preparing the boats."

An hour later the group took off. "What a great day, Joseph," Zach said. "We are so lucky to be allowed to be with Yeshua and the Twelve."

After two hours on the sea the boats turned for shore.

"James, look! I don't believe it. A huge crowd has followed us by land," John announced, furious at what he saw.

"I see them. It seems as though we will never have time out," said James, also quite annoyed. "I wonder what Yeshua will do now."

"It is a bit much not to allow you some time to rest, John," said Zach, who was adjusting a sail. "If I were you I would probably tell them to leave. At least before I met Yeshua I would have done that, or worse," Zach smilingly admitted.

"Yeshua, look at the crowd! It seems that we can't get away from them," Peter said.

"They are like sheep without a shepherd," Yeshua said quietly.

As Yeshua set foot on the shore, the crowd came forward to touch him and be near him, but the Twelve were able to get them to sit down so that he could speak to them. When they were seated Yeshua began to teach them, using stories, and puzzles, and arguments. Hour after hour he taught them.

"Where does he get the energy from, Zach?" Joseph quietly asked, knowing that he and Zach had already discussed this – but had come to no conclusion.

"I just don't know, Joseph. And where does he get such knowledge and such authority," Zach said as he watched, occasionally shaking his head in amazement.

"Master, it's already very late," said Judas, "and this is a lonely place. Send the people away and let them go to the nearby farms and villages in order to buy themselves something to eat."

Yeshua smiled. "You yourselves give them something to eat," he replied.

"Judas is entirely baffled at Yeshua's remark," whispered Joseph.

"Do you want us to go and spend two hundred denarii on bread in order to feed them?" replied Judas, thinking that Yeshua would see how impossible this would be.

"Joseph, if Judas is right, that amounts to two hundred days' wages for our workers. That's a large amount of money, but it is a huge crowd," observed Zach as he looked around at all the people.

"How much bread do you have? Go and see," Yeshua quietly said and Andrew went over to the baskets containing the provisions.

"Yeshua's words must have some other meaning, Zach," Joseph suggested. "There is no possibility that the food we brought in the boat could feed the thousands gathered here. In fact, I thought that we were going to buy food further on except that we were stopped by the crowd."

"I agree with you, Joseph. I wonder what will happen next," Zach said as he watched Yeshua calmly talking to Judas and the Twelve and waiting for Andrew to return.

"Master, I was only able to find five loaves and two fish," reported Andrew, with a small, questioning shrug, treating Yeshua's plan as hopeless.

"Ask the people to arrange themselves in groups on the grass," Yeshua instructed.

"Let's go," said Peter quickly, so that there would be no arguing among the Twelve.

James came over to Zach and Joseph. "You stay where you are. We are used to this," advised James, "though we have never faced this precise problem before."

In a very short time the Twelve had organised the people to sit down in groups of hundreds and fifties.

"Look, Zach, Yeshua has taken the loaves and fish and has blessed and broken them. What will happen next?" Joseph asked.

"Yeshua is asking the Twelve to give them to the people — it won't even feed the first row of the first group!" Zach muttered. "This is madness."

The Twelve went to the different groups.

"Where did they get enough to go around to each group?" asked Zach.

"They are still going round Zach... and still giving out bread and fish... how do you explain that?" said Joseph.

Zach, lost for words, whispered, "What's happening? Everyone seems to be happily eating. Just look at the children munching away. Joseph, what is happening, please tell me?"

"Well, if the seas and winds obey Yeshua, why not bread and fish?" Joseph replied with a broad smile.

"Some bread and fish for you," said John, as he handed the food to Zach and Joseph. Zach looked at the smiling face of his brother John, but was barely able to say thank you.

The two young men sat there and just watched everyone happily eating. Some were singing. Some of the children were playing together and laughing. Music came from one group and some more began dancing.

Yeshua was completely at ease, sitting quietly and watching the crowd. "Joseph, Yeshua is like the shepherd David spoke about in his psalm. If Stephen were here he could recite every line of it."

"I think you could too, Zach. In fact I am sure that you can," said Joseph.

Zach began

> "The Lord is my shepherd, I have everything
> I need. He lets me rest in fields of green grass. And
> leads me to quiet pools of fresh water.
> He gives me new strength.
> He guides me in the right paths as he promised.
> Even if I go through the deepest darkness I will not
> be afraid, Lord, for you are with me.
> Your shepherd's rod and staff protect me. I know that
> your goodness and love will be with me all my life.
> And your house will be my home as long as I live."

"I told you that you could, Zach," Joseph smiled.

Zach smiled, but then shook his head in disbelief and said, "Joseph, the Twelve seem to have full baskets of leftovers! That's impossible..." Then, in a very quiet voice, he continued, "Today something extraordinary has happened. Wait until Ruth and Stephen hear about this."

John came back over to the two pals, "Guess how many there were in the crowd?"

"I have no idea," replied Zach, "probably close to four or five thousand."

"Judas and Matthew, our mathematical experts, tell us that there were in the region of five thousand families," John smiled.

Just then James arrived. "John, Zach and Joseph, we have to get ready to go. Yeshua wants us to go to Bethsaida."

CHAPTER 15

"The sea is fairly rough tonight," said Peter, carefully eyeing the evening sky.

"I hope we don't end up in another storm," said Philip, trying to assess whether Peter was worried. If he was, things were bad. Peter, however, seemed content.

"And Yeshua decided to stay behind to make sure the people went home. I know he will cope but I would like to be there to help him," Peter added as he continued his rhythmic stroke of the oar.

"Don't worry, Peter, when Yeshua decides to stay behind then he already knows that everything will be okay," Philip said between breaths – he was getting tired. The wind blowing against them was becoming stronger.

"This wind is not helping. We've only gone a short distance, considering we have been a good few hours at sea already. James, is there any way we can increase our speed?" Peter asked.

"We are doing our best. Maybe if we turn a bit more North-North-East, we could make better time. But there is nothing in it," replied James, raising his voice a little to counteract the whistling of the wind.

"Is this as bad as it will get, or could it become worse?" Bartholomew asked, looking over at Philip.

"No, we often have nights like this, it's very unlikely it will get any worse," answered James. "It's just the direction of the wind that's the problem." Some spray came over the bow and landed on Philip. He smiled but his smile was a bit like watered milk.

"James, look over there! What is that?" Philip was pointing to a kind of pale figure seemingly walking on the water. Philip's face was white with fear, his eyebrows raised and his eyes bulging.

The Twelve stopped rowing and looked across at what appeared to be a person striding along the surface of the sea.

"I think it's a demon," one of the Twelve announced. A number of them were now standing – those who were not fishermen. One was holding a knife in his hand.

"Zach, do you see it?" asked Joseph, who was sitting beside him.

"I do, Joseph. It... is coming closer. I've never seen anything like this before... have you?" Zach answered. His face didn't reveal fear but rather a willingness to fight against anything that dared to hurt them.

"Never... but I think it is a man, Zach," Joseph whispered.

A voice spoke from the sea, "Courage! It is I. Don't be afraid!"

"It is Yeshua!" exclaimed John.

"It is Yeshua," Zach agreed, the aggression in his face replaced by wonder.

Peter was not convinced. He was standing and staring. "Lord, if it is you, command me to come to you on the water," he said.

"Come, Peter," said the figure.

Peter got out of the boat and started walking on the water. At first he seemed assured and very brave but then it was as if he woke up and realised that he really was walking on water. He looked down at his feet and the dark, deep water. His brave face now took on a look of terror.

"Save me!" he cried, as he raised both of his arms instinctively. He then half-threw himself towards Yeshua who lifted him up so that he was standing again.

"Oh you of little faith, why did you doubt?" Yeshua chided him with a gentle smile as they walked together to the boat.

"I think I would doubt too," whispered Zach to Joseph who was speechless. He had just seen his brother walking on the water. He began to think that he must be in the middle of a frightening dream, but the wind on his face assured him that he was not and that all this was real.

Happily, James took charge of the situation. He greeted both Yeshua and Peter with a hug and everyone relaxed. The group was again ready to row on, but the destination was changed to Gennesaret.

"That's nearer," murmured Zach to himself, "a good decision." And then to Joseph he said, "Wait 'til the others hear of this!"

"I don't know about you, Zach," replied Joseph, who was beginning to get his composure back, "but I have rarely been so scared in my life. It was nearly as bad as that time in the storm when Yeshua was asleep in the boat. At least in the storm I was busy bailing out water. In this case I was just looking at what I thought was a ghost or demon, or whatever, and felt helpless to do anything about it. And then Peter began to sink. I don't know what I would have done if my brother had been drowned. I certainly won't forget today."

When Yeshua and the Twelve arrived at the shore there was already a crowd and so the work continued for a short time. But in the end they managed to have some quiet time together.

"They are here again," said Zach.

Zach looked in bewilderment at the long-faced Pharisees. They were stern and spoke with sharp words. There was no respect in their voices.

"And Pharisees are good people," continued Zach. "They observe the Law better than anyone else. They even observe the very small laws about everyday eating and washing of hands. They also fast and pray and give alms. Wouldn't you think that they would be supporting Yeshua?"

"Why is it that your disciples do not follow the teaching handed down by our ancestors, but instead eat with ritually unclean hands?" they coldly inquired.

"Is that all they are worried about?" Ruth spoke in a barely audible voice to Zach.

"We have washed our hands, Ruth. Maybe it is not exactly the way required by ritual but our hands are clean," replied Zach.

Yeshua responded to his visitors, fearlessly and calmly looking straight at them eye to eye, never raising his voice.

"How right Isaiah was when he prophesied about you! You are hypocrites, just as he wrote, 'These people, says God, honour me with their words but their heart is really far away from me. It is no use for them to worship me because they teach human rules as though they were my laws!'"

"Zach, did you hear... 'Hypocrites'. They won't like that!" Ruth muttered.

"That's what they are. Only Yeshua has the courage to tell it as it is. We ordinary people are afraid to tell the truth to our leaders," Zach stated, beaming broadly.

The teachers of the Law and the Pharisees were taken aback. Their faces were furious, their eyes flaming with anger. If other people had not gathered to see what was happening, they would probably have begun shouting at Yeshua.

"How dare this carpenter from Nazareth say that about us," one muttered through his clenched teeth.

"He's only an uneducated sinner and blasphemer. Why should we worry?" sneered another with a disdainful expression.

But Yeshua was not finished with them. He continued, "You have a clever way of rejecting God's law in order to uphold your own teaching. Moses said, 'Honour your father and mother,' and, 'Anyone denouncing father or mother should be killed.' But you weasel out of that by saying that it's perfectly acceptable to say to father or mother, 'What I owe you I've given as a gift to God,' thus relieving yourselves of any obligation to your father or mother. And there are many other things like this that you do."

As the Pharisees stood there, with their flowing robes, their leather sandals and their long, stony faces, muttering to one another, Yeshua called over the local people who were already numerous and who had been listening to all this from a safe distance. "Don't you understand? Nothing that goes into you from the outside can really make you unclean, because it does not go into your heart, but into your stomach and then out of the body. It is what comes out of you that makes you unclean. For from inside, from your heart, come the evil ideas that lead you to do immoral and evil things, to rob, kill, commit adultery, be greedy, deceitful, indecent, jealous, and proud – all these evil things come from *inside you* and make you unclean."

"That is so obvious, Zach," Stephen said quietly but with noticeable joy. "At the same time it needed to be said. It certainly lifts a whole bunch of worries about ritual from my life that I now see were created by men and not by God."

"Another attack beaten back," said Joseph smiling, jumping and boxing the air, as the Jerusalem visitors disappeared up the road.

"That's all right," said Zach, as Stephen and Ruth were laughing at Joseph, "but remember John the Baptist. These men will be back with reinforcements. I think they are dangerous, like a pack of injured wolves. Beware of injured wolves. They can tear us to pieces."

After this confrontation, Yeshua decided to leave the area completely and, with the Twelve, went to Tyre and Sidon.

———————— ++++++ ————————

Meanwhile, one afternoon Zach and Ruth were passing a small school when the teacher, who was a follower of Yeshua, stopped them and asked them if they would tell his class one of Yeshua's stories. They happily agreed.

As they entered the classroom, all fourteen children got out of their seats and sat on the floor, crossing their legs at various angles. There was, as expected, some shoving and pushing to make sure they all had a good view of both Zach and Ruth. But it all stopped when Zach looked sternly at them and began, "Once upon a time there were two young men whose dad had two big farms. He was very wealthy."

"He must be very, very rich," Jotham, a boy in the front row, interrupted. Zach gave him a stern, if half-smiling, look.

"The second son asked his dad to sell one farm and give the money from the sale to him. His older brother could have the second farm. But of course their dad was not dead and normally the sons would not get anything before he had died. So the young man was really saying that he didn't mind if his dad was dead or not, he just wanted the money from the sale of the farm."

The children looked at each other disapprovingly, some even shook their heads. One was about to speak, but the child beside him told him to "shhh", putting his finger up to his mouth.

"Well, the dad did sell the farm and gave his younger son all the money he got for it. And not long after that the son left his father and brother and went to a country that was very far away. He was quite happy because his pockets were now full of money. As you can imagine, the young man, when he settled down in the new country, had a great time spending all his money... eating and drinking and sometimes he did bad things too."

"If he was a bad man he wouldn't be allowed back into the synagogue," a young boy called Asaph at the back of the group pointed out.

"Well," continued Zach, nodding to the boy, "after some time the young man had spent all his money, and as life would have it, a dreadful famine came to the country where he was, and it became hard to get any food. The young man knew then that he had to get a job or he would die of hunger. After much searching around, he did get a job... feeding pigs."

"Pigs? But, Zach, our people do not eat or even touch pigs," the little girl Sarah said, with a horrified look. She turned to the girl beside her who nodded her head in agreement.

"That is true, Sarah, but this young man did feed pigs. And he was still so hungry that he would have been happy to eat the food given to the pigs. But no one gave him any food."

"He must have been very hungry," a young boy, called Azor, said quietly.

Zach smiled and then said, "Ruth will now continue the story."

Ruth looked at the class with a look of suspense on her face. They all gazed at her.

"One day," continued Ruth, "the young man thought, 'I am being very stupid. On my dad's farm all the workers have enough to eat, in fact they have even more than they need and here am I starving. I will go back to my dad and tell him that I have sinned against heaven and before him. I am no longer worthy to be called his son, that he should treat me like one of his hired servants.' So he set off on his long way home."

"Ruth, how did he travel all that distance without food. He must have been very hungry and tired," Jotham, in the front row, asked.

"Oh yes Jotham, he was very hungry and tired. But he still walked and walked and walked. And then, when he was still a good way away from home, he saw a man running towards him."

"Was it a robber?" Azor asked, wide-eyed in wonder.

"No, Azor, the man who was running came up to him and put his arms around him and kissed him. Who do you think it was?"

The children looked at one another but no one could work it out.

"It was his dad," Ruth said.

"His dad?" the little boy Asaph in the back of the group said with surprise.

"Yes," said Ruth, "his dad had been looking out for his son every day and when he saw him in the distance, he ran all the way to meet him and hugged and kissed him. His son, however, said, 'Father I have sinned against heaven and before you; I am no longer worthy to be your son. Treat me like your hired servants.' But his dad just smiled and, with his arm lovingly across his son's shoulder, walked home."

"And when they got back to the farm his dad said to his slaves, 'Quickly bring out a robe – the best one – and put it on my son here; put a ring on his finger and sandals on his feet. And get the fatted calf and kill it, and let us celebrate; for this son of mine was dead and is alive again; he was lost and is found.' And they began to celebrate... Zach will continue." Ruth looked at Zach encouragingly.

Jotham, the little boy in the front said "Zach, his dad gave him sandals. Does that mean he had no sandals and walked all that distance?"

"That was clever of you to think of that Jotham, you are right. But was the young man's dad right to be so kind to his son, should he not have punished him severely?" asked Zach.

"Yes, he is a sinner so he should be punished for some time for the bad things he did. I wouldn't let him back to the synagogue," a young boy called Achim, standing up with his hands on his hips, strongly insisted.

"I don't know," said a girl called Miriam. "He was sorry for what he did. I think my dad would be very annoyed with me at first, but then he would forgive me."

"What about his mother? Would his mother forgive him?" Ruth asked a little girl in the front, who had a long face.

"I don't think so, because all the people in the town would know what he had done. They would think that his parents hadn't brought him up properly," said young Sarah.

"Well," continued Zach, after a nudge from Ruth, "they had a great feast and his dad was very happy indeed – but what about the brother who had stayed behind?"

The children were silent, waiting for Zach to continue. Receiving no answer he continued, "His brother, who was his older brother if you remember, was coming along the road to their house, and heard the music and saw the dancing. He called one of the slaves who worked on his dad's land and asked what was going on. 'Your brother has come home, and your father has killed the fatted calf, because he has got him back safe and sound.'"

"The elder brother became angry then and refused to join in the party. So his dad came out and asked him why he wouldn't come in. The elder son said, 'For all these years I have been working like a slave for you and I have never disobeyed your command, yet you have never given me even a young goat so that I might celebrate with my friends. But when this son of yours comes back, having spent all the money you gave him on bad living, you kill the fatted calf to make a welcome-home feast for him!'"

"Well, the father was really upset and he said to his eldest son, 'Son, you are always with me, and all that is mine is yours. But don't you see that we had to celebrate and rejoice because this brother of yours was dead and has come to life. He was lost and has been found.'"

All the children were silent, not knowing what to say.

"What did Yeshua mean by this story?" a bright young boy called Levi asked.

Zach smiled at the boy. "That is an excellent question, Levi. Yeshua was explaining to us that God is like the dad in the story. He really loves all his sons and daughters. And if they do bad things he still loves them and hopes and hopes and hopes that they will come to their senses as the young man in the story did, and give up the bad things they are doing. He also wants us all to be like the dad, not the elder son, and forgive our brothers and sisters and always love them, no matter what."

CHAPTER 16

One evening when Zach's friends had gone home and he was about to go to bed, he turned to his brother, "John, I have really wanted to ask you a personal question. You don't have to answer it, but I would really like to know something."

"Sure, Zach, ask away. I am at home so rarely these days that we hardly get time to talk together."

Zach smiled, delighted with the answer of his favourite brother.

"What do you really think about Yeshua?"

John's face lit up with a smile, but then he became reflective and for some time just looked at Zach and then into the fire that was burning and crackling in front of them. After a while he turned to Zach and spoke in a slow, measured tone.

"Zach, in my view, Yeshua is very, very special indeed... in so many ways. Above all, he seems to respect everyone he meets, including sinners and outcasts. He is happy just to be with people, helping them, supporting them and, when asked, curing them. And, yes, he has amazing powers. But you know all that already. And he tells people that God has forgiven them their sins. That does puzzle me – I mean how does he know for certain that God has forgiven them? His great desire, however, is that we all become childlike in our approach to God and believe in God's unbounded love for us, which includes forgiveness, and that we trust God at all times even when everything points the other way. That being said, Zach, he is a man just like us. He eats and drinks, he laughs and sometimes cries. He has to relieve himself like us all, he needs sleep, though he sleeps less than the rest of us and, instead, prays for long periods, especially at night. And you remember me telling you about the voice that was heard at his baptism 'You are my son, the Beloved, with you I am well pleased.'"

John then recalled the storm on the lake and chuckled, "How insignificant we all are, Zach, in comparison with Yeshua. You remember the wind and waves obeying him, the feeding of the five thousand families, the walking on the water, all the cures and exorcisms? God listens to his prayers. Yes, he is beloved of God." John stopped, but was obviously very happy inside.

"But John, what about Yeshua's attitude to the Pharisees and Lawyers? He certainly has been hard on them." Zach was watching his brother very closely.

"Yes, Zach, he is tough on the Pharisees and Lawyers but still, deep down, he really likes and respects them too. And even though in many ways they are good people, they are very stubborn. He has to do his best to convince them to change their misleading views about God and what God wants of them. Yeshua wants them to understand that God loves them personally, but they persist in their view that God is served by just keeping rules and regulations. We now know that that is not true. Yeshua wants us to accept that God is close to us and that we should love Him intimately and love one another and that includes loving sinners, which we all are. Yes, his words are strong – but you know well that we don't catch fish by just smiling at them!"

"Could Yeshua be more than a man?" Zach looked straight into John's eyes to study his reaction to that question. But John nodded, showing Zach that his question was a very good question and had to be asked.

"We have all been asking ourselves that question Zach, but I must admit that not one of us so far has been able to figure it out."

Delighted that his brother had been completely open with him, Zach told John what he thought. "If God were like Yeshua I could believe in God without any difficulty. However, my problem is with a God who punishes and kills people and who allows people to suffer so greatly with terrible pain, and loneliness, and serious debilitation... Think of the lepers."

John nodded in agreement and then added, "Yeshua has changed our lives. But we have still a long way to go."

CHAPTER 17

After a short stay, Yeshua and the Twelve were moving off towards Caesarea Philippi, in the territory of Herod Philip, Herod Antipas' brother. Not wanting to see Yeshua go, the gang got permission from their parents to travel with him and the Twelve. Caesarea Philippi was little more than a long day's walk north of Capernaum. Zach's mother, and Mary, a friend of hers from Magdala, also decided to join them.

As Zach had predicted, by evening the group had not reached the city, but they stopped for the night some distance short of it.

The following morning, Yeshua asked a most unexpected question.

"Tell me," he said, looking straight at the Twelve, "who do people say I am?"

Never before had he asked a question like this. Everyone looked at one another, stunned. They had no idea what to say. Zach and the gang looked around at the group of adults and wondered what would happen next. Yes, the Twelve had often argued and discussed it among themselves, as John had earlier told Zach. But now, somehow, they had to find an answer.

Philip was the first to reply, "Some say that you are John the Baptist." As he said that, he was only partly looking at Yeshua. In fact he was merely repeating what Herod Antipas had said. Joanna had reported earlier that Herod Antipas was sure that Yeshua was John the Baptist come back to life.

Then Thomas gave another view, "Others say that you are Elijah." Thomas looked inquiringly into Yeshua's eyes.

By this point the ice had been broken.

"Others say that you are one of the prophets," Bartholomew said and a few nodded at that.

The gang were surprised at all the variety of ideas. But then Yeshua asked an even more direct question which put them all on the spot.

"Who do *you* say I am?" Yeshua looked around at each one as he asked this question. He seemed to be asking, 'Have you worked it out yet?'

"Exactly," whispered Zach. "It is easy to quote what other people think and say, and avoid giving our own opinions – 'he said this' or 'she said that' or 'they think this or that'. Zach was delighted that a 'real' question had been asked.

"You are right, Zach, the question couldn't be more direct," replied Stephen as he carefully watched the Twelve. Each one seemed to be hoping that someone else would speak first.

"I think that the question is meant for my brother," suggested Joseph to the gang, who then turned and watched Peter. Peter was silent. He pursed his lips a little, all the time looking silently at Yeshua and considering the question.

"Joseph, this is a very important moment for your brother," murmured Ruth to Joseph who was beside her, as she watched Peter struggle to find the right words. But Peter's silence lasted only a few moments. Slowly, as he looked at Yeshua, Peter replied slowly but firmly,

"You... are... the Messiah!"

Yeshua looked at Peter and then smiled a little as if saying 'I thought as much, but what you say are words, the reality is far beyond you at this time.' Yeshua then turned to all the Twelve and with a certain pleading in his voice said, "Do not tell anyone about me."

"What did Peter mean?" puzzled Ruth. "Was he speaking of a Messiah, like David, a conqueror of nations? I don't think that Yeshua wants to be a conqueror like David."

"I think you're right, Ruth," Zach agreed and then held up his hand and said softly, "Yeshua is explaining something to the Twelve."

The group went silent. Zach happened to be nearer to Yeshua than the others so he could hear what was being said.

"What has Yeshua said, Zach?" asked Ruth. Ruth was alarmed at Zach's paleness and the small tear at the edge of his eye, which he quickly wiped away pretending it was a midge.

"He said that he has to suffer many things and be rejected by the elders and the chief priests and by the teachers of the Law."

"But that has been the way since the beginning," said Stephen, trying to console Zach. "The whole attitude of those in power towards Yeshua has been very hurtful. Think of all those visitors from Jerusalem…"

"Yes," said Ruth. "And remember what the visitor from Jerusalem said when he was walking along with the Herodians, just after the curing of the man with the withered hand? He said 'We will have to kill Yeshua of Nazareth! He is a danger to us all, and possibly a danger even to our nation.'"

"Well," said Zach, trying to seem calm, "Yeshua has just said that he will be killed. To hear Yeshua say that directly, straight out of his mouth, is terrible. Before today it was vague, uncertain and unreal, but now it seems very real and must be true, since Yeshua said it."

The three pals looked silently at him and began wondering what they could do. Was there any way of stopping such a thing happening? Surely the Twelve could do something.

"Yeshua did add something after explaining that he would be killed," said Zach, with a look as if there might be some hope after all. "Yeshua added, 'Three days later I will rise to life.'"

Just then something of a row started. Peter had taken Yeshua aside and was telling him that what he had said was not going to happen. Yeshua listened but then sternly said, "Get away from me, Satan! Your thoughts don't come from God but from human nature!" Yeshua, saying these words, had put his hands on Peter's shoulders and had looked into his eyes and kindly but resolutely shook his head, like a father talking to his son.

"Peter has obviously misunderstood Yeshua's message," said Joseph, concerned that his hero, his brother, could make such a mistake.

"Nonetheless, Joseph," murmured Zach, "it is obvious from the way Yeshua looked at him, that your brother remains his right hand man. Yeshua only wants to clearly drum into all our heads and hearts that he is not a Messiah of power and might, as David was, crushing all his enemies, but is a King of love and forgiveness, who will suffer."

And then Yeshua shocked the Twelve even more.

"If any of you want to come with me, you must forget yourself, carry your cross, and follow me."

"What does that mean?" asked Ruth, mystified.

"What type of cross can Yeshua be talking about, Stephen?" asked Zach.

"I know of only one type of cross, Zach, and you and I saw a number of them when we were near Jerusalem," Stephen replied.

"No! That can't be it!" gasped Zach, as he stared disbelievingly at Yeshua. Ruth then realised what Zach and Stephen were talking about.

"But crucifixion is horrific!" cried Ruth.

Then Yeshua spoke again, "For if you want to save your own life, you will lose it. But if you lose your life for me and for the gospel, you will save it."

Joseph asked his friends, "If many of those of our age are going the wrong way or doing bad things, will we be strong enough to keep to the right way?"

The gang said little for a while and then Zach quietly asked, "What Yeshua is saying is a huge challenge for us all. What do we reply if he asks us to carry our cross and follow him?"

CHAPTER 18

Two days later Yeshua, Peter, James and John, climbed Mount Hermon.

"James and Peter, have you ever seen such a sight? Galilee and our Sea seem so small from here, though you can still see how beautiful they are," said John between breaths, as he stood for a moment resting and enjoying the view from the mountain.

"It surely is beautiful. Look at Capernaum there – it is so tiny," James replied, as the three looked down at their town.

Then, when they turned around, they saw that Yeshua, who was just a stone's throw away from them, had somehow changed in appearance.

"Look, Peter! Look at Yeshua!" gasped James as they all fell to their knees in shock.

Yeshua's clothes had become a brilliant white.

"It's as though his whole person is full of light..." whispered Peter as he held his hands up to shield his face from the blinding light.

"And love," added John, who had half-turned as he looked at Yeshua standing there, radiant.

"Who are *they*? Look, there are two people talking to Yeshua. How did they get here?" wondered James.

"If you ask me, we are looking at Moses and Elijah," said John in a slow measured voice.

"I agree, John," said James, "but why, I can't say. I presume that Moses is the one on the right, dressed with flowing robes and very strong features. He is like a king."

"Yes!" replied John softly, not wanting anything to interfere with the moment.

"It's easy to see why tens of thousands of people listened to him when he asked them to change their lives and leave Egypt." James was really talking to himself. "It was an enormous task to lead all those people, but he did it."

Peter, meanwhile, was staring at the vision of Elijah. "Elijah's strength is of a different kind to Moses," Peter whispered. "His eyes look like they can see straight through people, right into the past and into the future. He certainly would be a very tough opponent."

Peter felt that he had to say or do something to express his overwhelming happiness at witnessing the event, so he decided to speak out.

"Teacher, how good it is that we are here! We will make three tents, one for you, one for Moses, and one for Elijah."

Just as he had finished speaking a cloud overshadowed them all. Peter saw it and was terrified. It reminded him of the sudden storm on the sea on that never-to-be-forgotten day. His heart started pounding and he broke out in a cold sweat. But then a voice spoke from the cloud, "This is my own dear son, listen to him."

At the sound of the voice, all three covered their faces. The voice was deep and gentle but was frighteningly different to any human voice they had ever heard.

They waited, and waited... and waited, and then all three, almost at the same time, looked over to where Yeshua had been speaking to Moses and Elijah – but only Yeshua was there. The cloud was gone. Moses and Elijah had gone. And Yeshua's garments were back to the way they were before anything happened, though his face was still full of light. They just stared with astonishment at Yeshua.

Would they say anything? They didn't in the end, and neither did Yeshua. And he gave no explanation as to what had happened but just began to make his way down the mountain.

As he went, he seemed to be really happy, and it was only when they had descended a good way that he spoke about 'rising from the dead' and that he would have to suffer. The three were taken aback. Yeshua then told them to say nothing about what they had seen or heard until after his 'rising from the dead'.

When Yeshua and the three arrived down from the mountain, the rest of the Twelve and many other disciples were there waiting for them.

However, they were surrounded by a crowd of people, including teachers of the Law.

Yeshua asked what all the fuss was about.

A man in the crowd, who had moved so as to be nearer to Yeshua, answered, "Teacher, I brought my son to you because he has an evil spirit in him and can't talk. Whenever the spirit attacks him, it throws him to the ground, and he foams at the mouth, grits his teeth and becomes stiff all over. I asked your disciples to drive the spirit out, but they couldn't."

Yeshua noticed that the young boy looked frail and very sickly. He was about seven years old. He appeared frightened and obviously had some kind of fall recently, as his face was bruised and there was a red gash on his chin. He was trying very hard to hide behind his mother.

"Yeshua seems very affected by the situation," said Zach, as he watched Yeshua's reaction to the parents and the young boy. Zach did not know at that time about Yeshua's wonderful experience on the mountain, and how now he faced once again arguments and trouble.

"How unbelieving you people are!" Yeshua said to the crowd, sounding tired. "How long must I stay with you? How long do I have to put up with you? Bring the boy to me!"

As the parents brought their son to Yeshua, the son still tried to hide behind them. Then he saw Yeshua looking at him, and immediately went into convulsions and fell to the ground, rolling in the dust, kicking and flinging his arms everywhere. The father and mother quickly bent down to their son and covered him with a cloak to keep him warm. The boy looked terrible and was now only half-conscious. Yeshua asked the parents how long the boy had been like this?

"Master, he has suffered from this all his life. Many times the evil spirit has tried to kill him by throwing him into a fire and into water. Have pity on us and help us, if you possibly can!"

Yeshua with compassion looked down at the pallid, convulsed, young boy and then quietly said to the father, "If you yourself can. Everything is possible for the person who has faith."

All their years of worry were in the father's desperate cry that broke the uncertain silence. "I do have faith, but not enough! Help me to have more!" the father pleaded.

"Look! Yeshua is putting his hand on the young boy's head," said Zach urgently, as he strained to hear what Yeshua was saying.

"Deaf and dumb spirit, I order you to come out of the boy and never go into him again!"

There was complete silence in the crowd. The only noise was that of the teachers of the Law pushing forward to get a better look at the child on the ground and, of course, a better view of Yeshua.

The father, hardly breathing, looked anxiously at his boy. The boy's mother put her hand up to her mouth and just stared at Yeshua, then at her child and then at her husband. The silent crowd stared with doubtful hope. The teachers of the Law had begun to frown with evident disdain.

But then, a moment later, like a bird flapping its wings to take to the air, the boy let out a terrible, frightening cry. Indeed, it was more like a scream. His whole body once again became convulsed, his face became contorted and his body rigid. Then, slowly, his body began to relax and become still, and his face became peaceful.

"It looks as if he has stopped breathing," whispered John to Thomas who was standing beside him.

"He looks dead, John. What now?" said Thomas, with a look of resignation.

Led by the teachers of the Law, some of the crowd began saying, "He is dead!"

"I knew the teachers of the Law were right," said one bystander. "Yeshua of Nazareth has gone too far this time," said another.

"How can a law-breaker and sinner do any good," said one of the lawyers with an authoritative sneer. "God will have nothing to do with such people. Just look at the proof. The boy is dead."

'What a mess you have made, Yeshua!' was written all over their faces. In fact they were about to start jeering and blaming the parents for believing in Yeshua when, to their utter disbelief, Yeshua bent down and tenderly lifted the boy up.

"Ruth, Stephen, Joseph, the boy's eyes are opening! Look, he is standing by himself without the help of Yeshua. He is alive, he is alive!" cried Zach, his voice getting louder and louder.

The boy wasn't sure where he was or what had happened, but his father and mother quickly took him into their arms, with tears flowing freely. As they lovingly clasped him tight, his pallid face began to show some colour, and his mother with a little cloth rubbed off some foam that had remained around his mouth. They knew then that their son was cured and was at peace with himself.

Meanwhile, the people watching, seeing the miraculous cure unfold, were in shock. They turned and asked one another, "How can this be? Where does he get this power? Where will all this end?"

The boy's mother and father, with tears of joy, finally found words, quiet words, and thanked Yeshua over and over. He lovingly embraced each of them. Then, going down on one knee, Yeshua looked into the eyes of the boy and hugged him.

Then something amazing happened. The child spoke. "Thank you, Yeshua. I knew that you could cure me," he said.

"Anne, our child has spoken!" the boy's father whispered to his wife. These were the first words the boy had spoken in his life. The boy remained in Yeshua's arms for a few moments and then Yeshua gently said to him, "Son, look after your father and your mother."

"I will, Yeshua," he replied.

Then Yeshua handed him back to his parents and, turning, he walked away with the Twelve and the other disciples.

"You know," said Ruth as she watched them go, "it was as if Yeshua had picked up a beautiful flower and respectfully handed it to the parents."

When the Twelve finally asked Yeshua why they had been unable to cast out the demon in the child, Yeshua explained, "Only prayer can drive this kind out, nothing else can."

It was only then that the Twelve fully realised how essential daily prayer was in following Yeshua's way of life.

CHAPTER 19

When finally the Twelve arrived back at Capernaum a meal was waiting for them in Peter's house. Deborah, Peter's mother-in-law, had prepared it. And when the supper was over and the group had settled down, they just sat looking at one another in silence.

"I heard that the Twelve have been discussing among themselves which of them is the most loyal follower of Yeshua," whispered Ruth, with a knowing smile. "You men are all the same."

"What's wrong with that?" challenged Joseph.

Yeshua turned to the Twelve. "Whoever wants to be first must place himself last of all and be the servant of all."

When Zach, Stephen and Joseph heard this, they were shocked. "Our ideas are so wrong in so many ways," Zach exclaimed.

"And if we win many times we begin to feel that we are better than the other person, not only in the game but in general," added Stephen. "We have so much to learn."

Yeshua called over a little boy, who immediately ran into his arms. He was a nephew of Peter and about three years of age.

"He doesn't realise how fortunate he is to be called over by Yeshua and have Yeshua put his arms around him," said Ruth.

"Whoever welcomes one of these children in my name welcomes me," said Yeshua, "and whoever welcomes me, welcomes not only me, but also the one who sent me."

As he spoke he looked with some disappointment at the Twelve.

"If anyone should cause one of these little ones to lose faith in me, it would be better for that person to have a large millstone tied around his or her neck and be thrown into the sea," he said, with great seriousness. The child looked into Yeshua's eyes and knew that Yeshua really cared about him, even though he was small.

"It seems to me that Yeshua somehow knows that children will be treated badly in the future. God help those who do so," said Ruth as she watched the expression on Yeshua's face.

CHAPTER 20

The Passover was only a little over three weeks away, and the gang decided to ask their parents if they could go up to Jerusalem for the feast. Yeshua had been part of their lives for three years, so they felt that their parents would agree. Zach and Stephen were both seventeen, Ruth was sixteen, while Joseph was just 'five years short of twenty.'

"Dad and Mum, since Yeshua and the Twelve are going up to Jerusalem, I really want to be with them, especially since Yeshua believes he may be captured and maybe even killed," Zach spoke with unusual anxiety in his voice. Both his parents noticed it. His mother said calmly, "Zach, we are not going to stop you going. In fact I think we are happy that you want to go. I, too, will be travelling to Jerusalem along with a few friends of mine."

Zach's Dad, in the deep, commanding voice that always gave Zach reassurance, added, "Zach, a large consignment of our fish will be taken to Jerusalem for the feast. So that means that I must remain here and organise it, even though I would really like to go and be with both of you and, of course, with James and John, but I am sure, Zach, that everything will be okay with Yeshua. He is an extraordinary and wonderful man, with powers that none of us can understand. Anyone who would dare to take on Yeshua would be very foolish indeed. Yes, he has had arguments with the authorities, but in my view all his opponents do is argue and get hot under the collar. I can't see any of our rulers turning on him in any violent way. Anyway, your brothers will be going with him. Those two brothers of yours will look after him well. And if they don't, your mother will stand up for him – and nobody will argue with her!" Zebedee smiled, as did Zach and Salome.

"James and John are well known in Jerusalem, Zach, through our business there," Zebedee continued, "so go and don't worry. God will look after you all."

Both Stephen and Ruth were also allowed to go, but Joseph had to remain at home because he had been unwell for a few weeks.

When Zach, Stephen and Ruth arrived at Peter's house, Joseph passed on the sad news, "I am sorry I can't go with you this year. My dad and mum feel that I am not well enough. I have to admit that they are probably right. Although I am much better this week, I have been fairly out of sorts for awhile."

Zach put his arm around Joseph. "Don't worry, Joseph, we'll fill you in when we get back."

"We'll really miss you," added Stephen, his hand on Joseph's shoulder.

"Yes, Joseph, and you'll be fully recovered when we return," Ruth assured him, giving him a hug.

Stephen's mother, Sarah, sat with Salome outside Zebedee's house. Like Stephen, she was a woman with pale features, dark brown eyes and black hair. She was much smaller than Stephen, who was almost as tall as Zach, but she was obviously physically strong and fit. Her voice had a kindness in it. It was as if a smile could break out at any time. She was, like her son, a happy person.

"Salome, where will we all stay in Jerusalem?" she asked.

"Well, Sarah," said Salome, who frequently visited Jerusalem, "I know Yeshua has friends in Bethany, near Jerusalem, and they have a large house. As well as that, the upstairs section of our shop, along with the adjoining house which we have there, will provide enough room for everyone. I would be delighted to have everyone staying there. My husband also bought a small house with an olive garden just outside the walls of Jerusalem. That house has a caretaker who lives there, but he only uses one room, which leaves two more large rooms available. We'll be fine."

"You are very fortunate to have such accommodation. It is so difficult to find anywhere to stay during the feasts... Have you any idea when we will be leaving for Jerusalem?"

"I am not sure. Mary of Magdala is going to join us, and she is expected to arrive here within the next few days. We will probably leave soon after she arrives... I presume you have met Mary."

"Oh Yes! She has been over to our house a few times. I don't know her background at all, but she seems to be a lovely person," replied Sarah.

"Yes, Mary is a wonderful, generous and loving person. They say that when she was younger she lived a different type of life. If so, since becoming a follower of Yeshua, she has changed completely. Yes, she is very special. I always look forward to her coming here. My sons tell me that she has great wisdom and a practical mind. She has been on a number of journeys with the Twelve."

CHAPTER 21

Yeshua, the Twelve, the gang, Salome, Sarah, Mary of Magdala and about eighteen others from Capernaum had already been on the road to Jerusalem for three days.

Not long after sunrise on the fourth day, a group of women, a few men and a large number of children approached the camp where Yeshua, and all those with him, had spent the night.

"These people probably want their children to meet Yeshua so that he can bless them," said Stephen to Zach and Ruth. Matthew, one of the Twelve, was doing his best to dissuade the people from coming nearer.

"The Master is on his way to Jerusalem," Matthew said, "and is almost ready to go. So I don't think we will disturb him now. He will bless your children at some other time."

The adults were about to withdraw with their children, but then they heard a voice. "Let the children come to me, and do not stop them, for the kingdom of God belongs to such as these." Yeshua smiled at Matthew, assuring him that it was no bother but rather a joy for him to greet the children and their parents.

When the group saw Yeshua, there was an immediate reaction. The children ran to him as quickly as they could, to see who could be the first to reach him. Before long they had surrounded him, all looking for his attention at the same time. Yeshua sat down on a rock and then told the adults, "I assure you that whoever does not receive the Kingdom of God like a child will never enter it."

The gang were watching the scene from a short distance away. "I have yet to work out what that means," frowned Zach. "Yeshua has said it a number of times before."

Yeshua then embraced the children, one by one, giving each of them his blessing. The last child wanted to hang on to his clothes and not leave. But, after a kiss on his forehead from Yeshua, he went back to his mother.

"Those children are so fortunate to have met Yeshua and received his blessing," said Ruth.

"You are so right, Ruth, but that makes us doubly blessed to be travelling with him to Jerusalem," Zach said, as he watched Yeshua bid farewell to the last family and then prepare to continue his journey.

The weather was hot that day, but the group made good time and saw some wonderful scenery.

"Zach, look! A man has just run up and fallen on his knees before Yeshua," said Ruth to Zach, who was looking at some birds on a nearby tree.

"Where? Oh yes, I see him... and, judging from his clothes and the jewellery he is wearing, he seems to be a wealthy man," Zach replied.

Somewhat out of breath, the young man cleared his throat and then, in a hurried manner, asked, "Good Teacher, what must I do to receive eternal life?"

"The man obviously believes in an afterlife, unlike the Sadducees, who profess that there is no life after death," said Stephen, smiling.

Yeshua bent down and lifted up the man from his kneeling position and said, "Why do you call me good? No one is good except God alone. You know the commandments: 'Do not commit murder; do not commit adultery; do not steal; do not accuse anyone falsely; do not cheat; respect your father and your mother.'"

The man replied, "Teacher, ever since I was young I have obeyed all these commandments."

At this, Yeshua put his hands on the man's shoulders and spoke to him with deep affection. "You need only one thing. Go and sell all you have and give the money to the poor and you will have riches in heaven; then, come and follow me."

"That's a great deal to ask," said Stephen.

The young man stared in disbelief at Yeshua, wondering if he was only joking. The look on his face said, 'You can't be serious! Is that what it takes... everything?' He looked at the ground and then back at Yeshua. He was lost for words.

"Maybe he thought that he could buy eternal life?" Zach murmured, while at the same time empathising with him.

In the end the man smiled sheepishly at Yeshua, gave a little bow, muttered a few words and then turned and walked slowly away, giving the ground a half-hearted kick as he went.

Zach stood there transfixed, surreptitiously wiping a tear from his eye. "Shame," he said. "What a shame. Yeshua offered the man the huge gift of discipleship, and yet he turned away."

"He didn't want to be a follower of Yeshua at such a cost," said Stephen, who was also upset at the outcome.

The gang then turned towards Yeshua who was shaking his head and seemed deeply disappointed. Then he said, "How hard it will be for rich people to enter the kingdom of God!"

The gang and the Twelve were quite taken aback. Yeshua continued, "My children, it is much harder for a rich person to enter the Kingdom of God than for a camel to go through the eye of a needle."

Ruth smiled at that, since Yeshua had used a well-known proverb to make his point. Zach turned to the other two and said with great seriousness, "Yeshua surely can't mean that it is impossible for a rich man to be saved. My father could be considered quite rich."

A few of those surrounding Yeshua said, "Who, then, can be saved?" Yeshua looked around at all those present and speaking kindly but very seriously told them, "This is impossible for human beings but not for God; everything is possible for God."

CHAPTER 22

"I love all the singing as we walk along," remarked Ruth.

"And why wouldn't you, Ruth? You have a beautiful voice," Zach announced encouragingly.

"The psalms of David are great," mused Stephen, addressing his remark to nobody in particular.

"Zach, look over there... Roman soldiers... Roman soldiers always worry me. They have done such terrible things in this country." Ruth took Zach's arm nervously as she said this. Her eyes never left the large cohort of soldiers, their shining armour flashing in the late-morning sun.

"Don't worry," said Zach. "They are only going up to Jerusalem for the feast. All the important people in our country, as you know, meet in Jerusalem for the Passover."

The group of soldiers shortly disappeared over the hill in front of them and it was as if they were never there, though the pounding of hooves could be heard for a while afterwards. Then slowly, the singing of the birds, the singing and the conversation of the travelling pilgrims took over.

"How long will we have to put up with the Romans in our country?" asked Stephen.

"I wouldn't give them another thought, Stephen," said Zach. "If some day we can do something about them I'm sure we will, but for now let's enjoy our day. Didn't Yeshua tell us that we have enough to think about each day without worrying about our tomorrows?"

Zach seemed happy in himself, and Ruth realised that the words of Yeshua were changing him. Indeed, all their lives and their thinking were being slowly transformed.

"Bad news, Zach," said Stephen. "Look over there."

Herod's soldiers were passing in the distance on another road. Evidently, they too were on their way to Jerusalem.

"Like I said, Stephen, all the important people will be there including that murderer Herod Antipas. His soldiers look so different to the Romans but, as we know, they are just as ruthless," Zach replied, with an expression close to disgust on his face.

"Zach, are you thinking about Machaerus?" Ruth guessed.

"How can I forget it?" said Zach.

When Herod's men had followed the Romans over the horizon, the group continued their journey towards Jerusalem.

"You know, Zach, seeing all these farms and vineyards with the families working hard and the children playing... and then in the evenings cooking our food on the fires... the songs and the laughter... and then our discussions – it is all so wonderful. I have rarely been so happy," confided Ruth.

"Neither have I, Ruth," agreed Zach. "Neither have I."

"Look," Stephen said, "Yeshua is stopping... and calling the Twelve."

The women in the group in no time organised themselves and began preparing something to eat. The gang were about to help them but Salome signalled to Zach and Stephen to take it easy, that all was under control.

So they both went to a spot a little away from everyone.

"Here's a great place to sit," said Zach... "Aren't we fortunate to be travelling with Yeshua and the Twelve!"

"I would say 'blessed', Zach. But think of it, we have been close to Yeshua for three years now. How many have had, or will have, such an opportunity again?" Stephen asked.

Yeshua was not speaking in private so they were able to hear what he was saying.

"We are going up to Jerusalem," said Yeshua, "where the 'Son of Man' will be handed over to the chief priests and the teachers of the Law. They will condemn him to death, and then hand him over to the Gentiles, who will make fun of him, spit on him, whip him, and kill him, but three days later he will rise to life."

Zach and Stephen couldn't believe what they were hearing. "What does that mean, Zach? Look, the Twelve are really upset," Stephen spoke calmly, but his face betrayed his anxiety.

"It does sound ominous. Yet, Yeshua seems to have no hesitation in facing whatever is about to happen," replied Zach.

"On the other hand, Zach, Yeshua did add that he would rise again after three days, whatever that means," said Stephen.

"It's all too difficult for us and, if we start worrying about the future, we might become very frightened," cautioned Zach.

"Maybe we shouldn't have listened at all," Stephen suggested and then looked back at the camp, realising that the food was ready. "You're right Zach, I'll try to enjoy today and wait for the problems of tomorrow to reveal themselves. Hopefully, when they do, we will be able to deal with them."

CHAPTER 23

"The fields are narrow here, it must be easy to lose a sheep that strays," said Ruth as she looked at the plains and the encroaching desert.

"That's why shepherds often go in groups and look after their flocks together. There's safety in numbers," explained Stephen.

Just then a mournful wailing began echoing in the valley. Ruth looked startled. She quickly turned to Zach and Stephen. "What is that wailing? Listen!"

"Don't worry, Ruth, that's only some jackals. They generally go where people have been, and not to where people are. They are scavengers. The ones you need to watch out for are the wolves and very occasionally a lion," Zach smiled reassuringly at Ruth.

"Do shepherds have to listen to that every night?" she asked.

"It's nothing, Ruth, if only you knew," Zach began, and then decided to say no more. Stephen, however, continued to explain.

"The problem, Ruth, is that a shepherd is responsible for each sheep and has to account for it if it gets lost. Sometimes that means bringing home a dead carcass. That's one of the unpleasant things about being a shepherd. And some of the sheep are stubborn and need a rap of the crook to obey the shepherd. They just don't recognise danger. Sometimes shepherds actually die trying to save their sheep. One was mauled by a lion last year, but that's very rare. It is, as Zach said, mostly wolves that do the damage. But they won't attack us here since there are too many of us."

At that moment Ruth was distracted. "I don't believe it!" said Ruth. "Some teachers of the Law and some Pharisees are among those people who are coming towards us. They are probably from the local town."

"If they attack you, Ruth, I'll beat them off," Zach announced teasingly. Ruth looked at him and smiled.

They wandered over towards Yeshua and the others. Someone asked Yeshua to explain what God's love was like. He sat down on a rock, looked around at the pastures that surrounded the camp, where flocks of sheep were grazing, and began to speak softly.

"There once was a shepherd who had one hundred sheep. One day he finds that one of them is lost. So he leaves the ninety-nine and goes off after the lost sheep. When he finds it, rejoicing, he lays it on his shoulders, and brings it home. Then he calls his friends and neighbours together, saying to them, 'I am so happy I found my lost sheep. Let us celebrate!'"

Yeshua explained how the lost sheep symbolised a sinner and how God would go after a sinner in order to bring that sinner home to himself.

The group seemed delighted with the story.

"Did you notice Yeshua said 'when' and not 'if' he finds the sheep," remarked Zach. His two friends nodded. "Zach notices everything," Ruth admiringly whispered to Stephen.

Someone then asked about the danger for the shepherd and the many problems he may face. Yeshua answered with various explanations and examples, but then added, "I am the good shepherd who is willing to die for my sheep."

"There it is again," Zach spoke in a low voice. "Yeshua is warning us again."

Yeshua continued, "As the Father knows me and I know the Father, in the same way I know my sheep and they know me. And I am willing to die for them. The Father loves me because I am willing to give my life in order that I may receive it back again. No one takes my life away from me. I give it up of my own free will. I have the right to give it up, and I have the right to take it back. That's what my father has commanded me to do."

Zach shook his head at the constant mention of impending death. He looked over at the teachers of the Law and Pharisees and saw that they were annoyed.

Yeshua added, "There are other sheep which belong to me that are not in this sheep pen. I must bring them, too. They will listen to my voice. And they will all become one flock with one shepherd."

"You were right, Zach," said Stephen. "Yeshua couldn't be clearer about dying and what you said seems also to be absolutely true – that Yeshua is here for more than just our people. I believe his message is for all people."

CHAPTER 24

After five days Yeshua, the Twelve and the pilgrim group were close to Jericho, a city of a few thousand inhabitants and the gateway to Judea.

"Isn't this where Joshua entered Judea with our people, killing all the inhabitants?" said Ruth looking across towards the river Jordan.

"You're right," Stephen agreed. "It's also close to where our King David hid when he was being hunted by King Saul. And, Zach, didn't John tell you that it wasn't too far from here that Yeshua spent a long time praying and fasting after his baptism by John the Baptist?"

"That's true, but this place also has a bad name for robbers. Do you remember the story Yeshua told about a man going from Jerusalem to Jericho who met some robbers. Do you recall it? He was robbed and very badly hurt and could have died if he had been left on the road." Zach was re-imagining the event.

"I remember," said Stephen. "Didn't a priest and then a Levite pass by and ignore him? And we said that they probably didn't help him because they thought he might be dead and if they touched him they would become ritually unclean... look, a gravestone up ahead."

"It's hardly the grave of the man in the story," Zach teased, but then he became serious. "It always annoys me to think that both the priest and Levite left a man to die so that they could remain ritually clean. And, it was a Samaritan, a people we're taught to disregard and despise, that finally saved him. The Samaritan lifted him up and put him on his donkey, and then brought him to an inn and paid for his care until he got better. We are still so far from really knowing what practical love is and then actually practising it!"

As the pilgrim group came closer and closer to Jericho, they could see the river Jordan in the distance. It was only a short distance to the east. To the south the river ran into Lake Asphaltites.

"I am really looking forward to seeing Jericho," Ruth said with infectious enthusiasm. "It's meant to be a beautiful place, and have plenty of fresh water. I want to drink gallons of it."

"I hope there's enough for everybody," Zach joked.

"We should be there soon. It is probably over the next hill," Stephen remarked as he adjusted the bag on his shoulder.

On reaching the top of the hill they could see Jericho there in front of them in the distance.

"So that is Jericho," said Ruth.

"And there seems to be a welcoming party for you, Ruth," Zach teased. Of course they knew the crowd had gathered to see Yeshua.

However, as the gang got nearer they noticed a blind man on the side of the road. When the blind man heard the gang chatting together he asked them in a loud voice, "Why are all the people so excited?"

Ruth explained, "Yeshua of Nazareth is with us and is on his way to Jerusalem."

The man immediately, with the help of his stick, stood up.

"Tell me, how far away is the Prophet from where I'm standing?" he asked.

Stephen looked around and answered, "About forty feet or so."

With hope lighting up his face, the blind man let out a shout, "Yeshua! Son of David! Have mercy on me!"

He had a very strong, high-pitched voice, so despite all the noise made by the people, his voice could be heard clearly.

But someone from the crowd admonished him, "Bartimaeus, keep quiet! Don't annoy the prophet, he is on his way to Jerusalem."

Two other men said, "Shut up!"

The blind man stopped and pulled a face in the general direction of those who were discouraging him.

"Shout again, Bartimaeus," urged Zach. "I'm sure he will help you if you really want him to."

The man smiled with delight and shouted again, "Son of David, have mercy on me!"

Yeshua heard Batrimaeus then and called him.

"Bartimaeus, great news! Yeshua is calling you," Zach said. With his stick tapping the ground in front of him, Bartimaeus went trustingly with Zach and Stephen to Yeshua.

Bartimaeus was a short man, stocky and broad-shouldered. The clothes he wore were shabby and his sandals were broken so that one sole dragged along the ground. Because he was blind, he was unaware of his appearance.

When Zach and Stephen introduced him, Yeshua put his arms on the man's shoulders and speaking to him with his clear, deep voice said, "What do you want me to do for you?"

Yeshua was not just going to cure his blindness without being asked. Maybe it was something else the man wanted. Yeshua never acted unless he was certain what the person wanted. On one occasion a woman came to him who was very ill herself, but what she wanted was that her child be cured. Yeshua had asked her if she too wanted to be cured but she didn't seem to have thought about that at all. He cured both the mother and her child.

Bartimaeus answered, "Teacher, I want to see again."

"Zach, he must have been able to see at one time," Ruth suggested. She was standing beside Zach and Stephen.

The crowd had become very quiet and were watching intently. Yeshua, looking at Bartimaeus with great affection, gently said, "Go, your faith has made you well."

"Go?" Bartimaeus questioned – and then it happened. Suddenly he saw Yeshua standing in front of him, smiling. He returned the smile with a look of amazement. He looked left and right and up to the sky, and then left at a tree where a bird was singing.

"I can see, I can see again," he shouted, and then screamed it out for all to hear. "I can see again! I can see again!"

Turning to Yeshua, he slowly knelt down and held his healer's hands in his, kissing them. Yeshua smiled at Bartimaeus and, giving him a gentle tap on his shoulder, told him that he could join him on the journey to Jerusalem. Bartimaeus was overwhelmed. One of the women told him not to worry about clothes since there were clothes to spare among the Capernaum group that would fit him. Zach took out his spare sandals, "Bartimaeus, these might be better than yours. Ruth here noticed that yours were broken." Zach handed him the sandals.

"Oh thank you..."

"I am called Zach. It's good to meet you, Bartimaeus," said Zach. Bartimaeus looked at him and then turning to Ruth said, "And you, then, are Ruth. I am so happy to meet you." Ruth greeted him courteously.

"And this is Stephen," said Zach.

"Stephen, I am very happy to meet you," said Bartimaeus.

"And we are all delighted that you will be coming with us to Jerusalem," said Stephen. And so the group continued into the town and organised accommodation for the night.

The following day there was a great feeling of expectancy. They were getting closer and closer to Jerusalem and soon they would see it.

"It is such a wonderful feeling to be near Jerusalem and just waiting for it to appear in the distance," said Zach. "It reminds me of the times when I was young, waiting for my dad and our boats to come into the harbour... And then, when my father would wave to me and my brothers, we all cheered. Yes, waiting to see Jerusalem is just like that."

"I wonder will there be any changes since the last time we were here?" Stephen mused. "Will the Temple be as splendid and awe-inspiring as it was last year?"

"I'm sure it will," said Zach. "Mind you, it's difficult to believe that Solomon's Temple was even more magnificent than the one we have now. I often wonder what made the Babylonians destroy something so amazing."

"Where did Herod the Great get the money to build the present Temple?" asked Ruth.

"Guess, Ruth," Zach frowned. "Taxes and extortion."

"My dad told me that Herod the Great had ten thousand skilled men as well as one thousand priests working on the Temple, so that the sanctuary could be built," said Stephen. "Only the priests were allowed to work on the sanctuary. They must have worked very hard since they built the sanctuary in less than two years, while the outer courts took eight years to finish. Imagine paying all those people for eight years! And even after eight years the work still wasn't finished. The whole Temple and its surrounds, with all its delicately-designed gates and other furnishings, took longer. Yes, sacks of money were required."

"But Stephen, I think it was all worth it," Zach said with a smile. "We will remember our visits to Jerusalem for our Jewish feasts our whole lives. To see and hear the crowds and to be involved in the ceremonies and the singing is fantastic. Each time I visit Jerusalem it seems more exciting than the previous time and, of course, I am getting older and can understand and appreciate it more."

Just before reaching the hill where Jerusalem could be seen, John came over and told Zach and Stephen that Yeshua wanted to speak to them. Delighted, but wondering why, they immediately ran over to Yeshua. He just smiled in his usual way and said, "Stephen and Zach, I was wondering if you could go ahead of us into that village?" They both nodded that they would. "And as soon as you get there, you will find a donkey tied up that has never been ridden. Untie it and bring it here. If someone asks you, 'Why are you doing that?' just say this, 'the Master needs it and will send it back at once.'"

"Of course, Yeshua," they replied.

Immediately they set off, running most of the way on the sandy road. Just before entering the town Stephen, almost out of breath, asked, "What happens Zach, if the people in the village think that we're stealing the donkey?"

"I've no idea," Zach replied.

Then they looked at one another and laughed and shrugged their shoulders. They trusted that Yeshua knew what he was doing.

Soon they arrived at the village and sure enough there, tied up in front of them, just beside the door of one of the houses in the main street, was a lively young donkey.

"It seems to be expecting us," said Zach. The donkey looked sideways at them, shook its head and then brayed loudly. As they untied it, Stephen said quietly, "I feel as though I am taking something without permission."

There were three men standing close by engaged in conversation. But when the donkey brayed, they all looked over at the two 'robbers' questioningly. One of them – a large, red-faced man with a grey beard – turned and pointed at them saying, "Are you tricksters or petty thieves or what?"

"What did he say, Zach? I can't understand his accent," said Stephen.

"Neither can I. Keep going," urged Zach.

Then another member of the group, a rather tall and strong looking man with bushy eyebrows and a stern face asked them, "What are you doing untying that donkey?"

The boys looked at each other. This time they understood what was said. "The Master needs it and will send it back at once," replied Zach, as Yeshua had told them.

At that, the men smiled and nodded, seeming quite happy with the reply.

"The men must know Yeshua," said Stephen, relief all over his face.

"I would say it's the same all over Judea and Galilee," agreed Zach, as he settled the donkey.

On their way back they considered taking turns riding the donkey, but since Yeshua had said that the donkey had never been ridden before, they decided that Yeshua should be the first.

Soon they had reached the Twelve and John took charge of the donkey and brought it to Yeshua. When he saw it he smiled and thanked Zach and Stephen.

"The donkey seems so tame, as if it is used to obeying orders and carrying loads without complaint," said Zach.

When they had all tidied up and were ready to move on, a few of the Twelve threw their cloaks on the young donkey for Yeshua to sit on. Yeshua smiled and patted its head. Everyone gave a great cheer. Then, as the donkey began to move forward, Ruth commented, "Doesn't Yeshua look so gentle, and really happy on the donkey? He is so different to the Roman soldiers who always look so arrogant and aggressive on their large and fearsome horses."

As the donkey with its very precious cargo made its way along the road, a number of the group were so touched by the scene that they began to throw their cloaks on the road in front of Yeshua. These were followed by branches and greenery taken from the trees and fields nearby. Then, as the procession reached the downward slope of the Mount of Olives, they all began to move a little faster and began singing. One of the songs they sang was Zach's favourite.

"Give thanks to the Lord, because he is good, and his love is eternal

Let the people of Israel say, 'His love is eternal.'

My God bless the one who comes in the name of the Lord...

With branches in your hands, start the festival and march around the altar."

At one stage, Zach turned to Ruth and said, "You know, Ruth, all this singing and rejoicing makes me feel like I have just landed a large catch of fish after a long night without success."

Some of the group walked ahead and began jumping around as they sang. One or two even turned cartwheels. Needless to say, crowds of people were watching them as they travelled cheerfully along the road.

"Look, Zach," said Ruth, almost out of breath. "Look who's watching us."

"Pharisees?" exclaimed Zach, as he turned to where Ruth was looking. "And they seem to be annoyed at something. What do you think?"

"I agree," Ruth replied with a shrug. "But what can they do?"

The Pharisees had reached Yeshua and were walking along beside him. Their elegant robes looked quite out of place beside the well-worn clothes of Yeshua who was still sitting on the donkey. And their long faces were such a contrast to the happy, peaceful face of Yeshua. Eventually, one of them said in a loud voice, "Teacher, command your disciples to be quiet."

"Did you hear that?" said Stephen, grinning broadly. "No chance!"

The gang then moved closer to hear what Yeshua would say. He calmly replied, "I tell you, if they keep quiet, the stones themselves will start shouting."

So delighted were the gang at Yeshua's reply that they threw their arms around one another as they walked along. The Pharisees were speechless.

"The Pharisees seem so angry at Yeshua," said Stephen.

"He is so open with them," said Zach, "but they are far from open with him. They have so much hidden, unspoken anger. They could be considered the enemy and a very dangerous enemy at that. Fortunately, Yeshua can always outwit them and beat them in an argument."

"Zach, let's forget about them," said Ruth. "Let's enjoy today, as you have often said. Yeshua will look after tomorrow." Smiling she linked Zach's arm and together they joined the group who were still singing and rejoicing.

Then, as they came over a hill Zach shouted, "There it is, Ruth! Jerusalem!" He could hardly believe his own delight at seeing the city. It was more magnificent than he had remembered. The whole pilgrim group let out a series of joyful shouts. In no time a song started up and everyone joined in enthusiastically.

"You see now, Ruth, why Stephen and I love coming here," Zach's face was beaming with happiness. "We are so lucky that God chose our people to be his own." Then he looked over at Yeshua.

"Ruth, Stephen," he spoke in dismay, "Yeshua is crying, and I don't think his tears are tears of joy..."

"He weeps sometimes when he meets some terrible cases of suffering," Stephen added. "But why cry now, in front of mighty Jerusalem, the pride of our people?"

"And particularly as the Temple of God comes into sight," whispered Ruth, holding tightly onto Zach's arm. Stephen moved closer to them both and stood beside them quite taken aback at the scene.

"I feel like crying myself now," said Ruth.

Then Yeshua spoke. He spoke in a voice that sounded as if he were uttering a terrible prophecy.

"If you only knew today what is needed for peace! But now you cannot see it! The time will come when your enemies will surround you with barricades, blockade you, and close in on you from every side. They will destroy you completely and all the people within your walls. They will not leave a single stone in its place, because you did not recognise the time when God came to save you!"

"This is horrific," said Stephen. "Is Yeshua talking about the Babylonians, many centuries ago?"

"It sounds to me as though he is speaking about something that is going to happen soon," Zach suggested.

"Look," said Stephen, "the Twelve, like us, don't know what to make of it."

Meanwhile, the women of the group, practical as always, began discussing what to do next. Salome suggested they start preparing the evening meal.

"Your mother is organising supper," Ruth said to Zach. "The decision has been made to stop a little early and eat before going into the city. I must go and help them."

117

"You know, Stephen," said Zach, "it really feels as though we have been going up and down hills. A very short while ago we were utterly delighted, singing and walking towards Jerusalem, longing for a glimpse of the great city with all its ramparts, its huge walls and amazing Temple. And then we see it, and it is as if we have arrived in a valley of tears and great sadness... Let's give Ruth and the others a hand."

Yeshua and some of the Twelve did not wait to eat. They continued on into the city and went into the Temple area for a while. However, they stayed the night in Bethany with their friends, while the rest of the pilgrim group went on to Zebedee's houses in the lower city.

PART 2

JERUSALEM 30 CE

CHAPTER 25

"This is a lovely house, Zach, with plenty of room for everyone. You are so lucky to have a place like this in Jerusalem," Ruth enthused as she was given a room along with Salome, Mary of Magdala and Joanna.

Zach and Stephen had their own little space over the shop section of the building. As they settled down to go to sleep, Stephen turned to Zach. "What a day," he said. "I will never forget it. I still wonder what Yeshua meant by what he said about Jerusalem."

"None of us will forget it," Zach replied. "Interestingly, Ruth reminded me earlier of another story that Yeshua told us some time ago, I don't know if you remember it. It was about a fig-tree."

"No, I didn't hear it, Zach, what was it about?"

"There were some Pharisees and teachers of the Law there at the time so it may have been aimed at them. Anyway, the story goes like this, there was once a man who had a fig tree growing in his vineyard. He went looking for figs on it but couldn't find any. So he said to the gardener, 'Look, for three years I have been coming here looking for figs on this tree and I haven't found any. Cut it down! Why should it go on using up the soil?' But the gardener answered, 'Leave it alone, Sir, just one more year. I will dig around it and put in some fertilizer. Then if the tree bears figs next year, so much the better. If not, then I will cut it down.'"

"You know, Zach," said Stephen, "Yeshua, as in the story of the fig tree, has been with us for nearly three years."

"True...," mused Zach. "So do you think the fig tree could symbolise Jerusalem?"

"I think it could. Maybe now that we are here, Yeshua will finish the story," Stephen looked at Zach with great seriousness.

"I hope we'll be able to sleep tonight Stephen," Zach remarked, remembering that at times like this he often experienced nightmares.

The following morning all three of the gang admitted that they had slept badly but at least they had had no nightmares. Then, after having prayed together and breakfasted rather quickly, they decided to join the Twelve at Bethany. However, on the way, Ruth pointed to a group approaching them.

"I think that is Yeshua and the Twelve coming towards us," she said.

"Yes, it is Ruth," replied Stephen, "but have you ever seen such crowds? Zach! Mind that sheep behind you."

Zach smiled. "In this crowd of people and all these animals, it would be easy to get lost or trampled or pushed out of the way. We had better keep close together."

"Zach, Yeshua has stopped near that fig-tree," Ruth said as they nudged their way through the crowd to get closer.

"Yeshua seems upset and is looking at the fig tree to see if there is any fruit on it," Stephen said. His two pals stopped and watched what was happening.

"It's the wrong time of year for figs," Zach observed.

"No one will ever eat fruit from you again!" Yeshua told the tree.

"Did you hear that, Zach and Stephen?" Ruth asked.

But Stephen turned to Zach and said, "There is your answer, Zach. I am afraid that our trip to Jerusalem will mark, in some way, the end of the fig tree. And the fig tree, no doubt, represents Jerusalem. Maybe it's something to do with the way our leaders live by law and not by love, and won't listen to Yeshua."

"Ruth, Stephen and I were discussing the story of the fig tree we heard some time ago," Zach said.

"I remember it well," she replied. "There was no proper end to the story. Yeshua didn't say what the owner of the fig tree finally did."

"I think that we are dealing here with symbols," said Stephen. "Do you remember the story of Jeremiah when he, like Yeshua, was near Jerusalem, and he took a flask and told people that God was going to bring great evil on Jerusalem? And then he broke the flask as a sign of what would happen?"

"Yes indeed," replied Zach. "In time, Nebuchadnezzar took all the treasures of Jerusalem, captured the king and ten thousand officers and chief men, and carried them off in captivity to Babylon for seventy years."

"Do you think God would punish his people?" asked Ruth, practical as ever. Her two friends were silent then for some time as they thought about her remark.

"I don't think Yeshua's God would punish his people unless it would help them in some way," Zach proposed.

"So what will happen?" asked Ruth.

"Maybe the teachers of the Law, the Pharisees and our elders will bring it all upon themselves," suggested Zach, "and God will allow it to happen to teach them a lesson. A very, very hard lesson. But our people will learn from it and grow as God's people. And, meanwhile, the Pharisees and elders, the lost sheep, will be carried home on the back of the 'true shepherd'. "

"I believe," added Stephen, "that whatever Yeshua says, will happen in due course, but it will be terrible for those living in Jerusalem when it does happen."

"On the other hand," said Zach, seeing that Ruth was getting very worried, "the fig tree was still fully alive after Yeshua had spoken to it."

"And have you noticed, Ruth," Stephen addressed her with care, "that when Yeshua is around, nothing bad happens to us? Even the raging winds and angry waves obeyed him and no one, no matter how smart or important they were, ever beat him in an argument."

"You are so right, Stephen," agreed Zach emphatically.

After a rest, the gang were ready to enjoy the remainder of the day in the city, but just then Yeshua and the Twelve arrived, explaining that they were going to the Temple. The gang decided that they would like to join them and soon they were on their way.

"Zach, Stephen... look at Yeshua! He has just turned over two tables of the money-changers! Money is rolling all over the ground!" Ruth cried.

"The money-changers are not too happy. Listen to their language... that's not acceptable in the Temple," said Stephen disapprovingly.

"Look," said Zach, "Yeshua is angry. His presence, like with the waves and wind, is enough to cool them down. Mind you, when you think about it, the money-changers must have been given permission to be here ... Whoever gave it hasn't much understanding of the sacredness of the Temple, and I suppose neither have the money-changers."

"What a mess!" Stephen was watching one money-changer in particular as he spoke. "Look at that man running after his money on the ground, and cursing as he goes!"

"Yeshua is not finished! He's now knocking down the chairs of the dove-sellers... " Ruth said, and added happily, "but he is not harming the birds themselves."

"I have a terrible feeling that the people who are behind this money racket will want revenge," murmured Zach.

Only then did the other two grasp the full extent of what was happening.

"It is written in the Scriptures," Yeshua's voice loudly and clearly rang out, "that God said, 'My Temple will be called a house of prayer for the people of all nations.' But you have turned it into a hide-out for thieves."

"The people are nodding in agreement," Zach said delightedly.

"But not the teachers of the Law and the Pharisees," Stephen noted, and the gang turned their attention towards them.

"Look! Some blind and lame people have arrived," said Ruth, "and I think that Yeshua is praying over them and healing them."

"It shows that people know that Yeshua is really special and that God's power is in him," Stephen smiled to himself as he said this.

"I think it's time to go home," suggested Ruth.

Having looked at the sun, which was now low in the sky, they all agreed and left.

CHAPTER 26

The following morning the fig tree was dead.

"What happened to the tree?" one onlooker said, shaking his head. "I've never seen anything like this before. It was perfectly healthy yesterday and now today it is dead."

"Zach, what does this mean? It scares me," Ruth spoke quietly.

"Stephen was right," said Zach, his eyes meeting Stephen's, and then looking across at the dead tree, as if he were looking not merely at the tree but into the future. "Stephen, you said that if anything happened to this fig tree it was a clear sign of serious problems to come."

"I did," said Stephen, looking very concerned. "Even so, I have no idea what these problems might be."

"And obviously, Stephen, this sign is not merely for us, but for everyone coming and going along the road... Those Pharisees and teachers of the Law over there are also studying it carefully," Ruth's voice shook as she spoke.

"Yeshua deliberately picked this tree since it is in a prominent place and visible to all," Zach said, thinking aloud. "Fully alive yesterday, completely dead today – a frightening sign. What is Yeshua telling us?"

The gang then saw Yeshua and the Twelve coming up the road towards them. When they arrived, Peter saw the tree. He looked as if he had seen a ghost. Immediately, he turned to Yeshua,

"Look, Teacher, the fig tree you cursed has died," Peter said.

Yeshua looked at the tree for some moments in silence and then said, "Have faith in God. I assure you that whoever tells this hill to get up and throw itself into the sea and does not doubt in his heart, but believes that what he says will happen, it will be done for him. For this reason I tell you: when you pray and ask for something, believe that you have received it, and you will be given whatever you ask for. And when you stand and pray, forgive anything you may have against anyone, so that your Father in heaven will forgive the wrongs you have done."

Zach listened with unbroken attention and then he turned to Stephen and Ruth, "We often say that 'faith could move mountains', that it can remove the greatest obstacles we come across in our lives that stop us from being good people. I think Yeshua is asking us to have a faith that I certainly don't have."

"And when we pray to forgive people completely, that is really hard," added Ruth. "Didn't he once tell Peter to forgive people 'seventy times seven times'?"

"What a memory, Ruth! You are absolutely right," Zach said, as the three followed Yeshua and the Twelve along the road to the Temple.

"Here they come," Stephen nudged Zach and Ruth as he pointed out some chief priests, teachers of the Law and elders coming through a gate and walking towards Yeshua.

"Someone had to complain about yesterday's cleaning out of the Temple," Stephen chuckled to himself.

"And maybe the death of the fig tree today," added Zach.

One of the richly-dressed group addressed Yeshua. He was tall, with a long grey beard and a large mouth. His head was covered with a cone-shaped headdress made of linen wrapped around many times. It had a plate of pure gold attached. His sumptuous robes were enriched with costly dyes, golden threads and precious stones. He was very impressive looking. Unfortunately, there were no kind words, no words of respect, no hint of acceptance of Yeshua as he began haranguing him, "What right have you to do these things? Who gave you such authority?"

A crowd had gathered and the conversation was deliberately in public for everyone to hear.

Yeshua looked calmly at the group, who stood there questioning him, and slowly replied, "I will ask you just one question and, if you give me an answer, I will tell you what right I have to do these things... Tell me, where did John's right to baptise come from? Was it from God or from human beings?"

The man and the group of questioners with him just stood there and stared at Yeshua. Then they turned to one another and began to discuss among themselves. There was a certain fury in their faces and gestures.

"I think they are afraid of Yeshua," said Ruth.

"I think you're right," Zach whispered back. "If only they knew him."

"Zach, why are they not answering Yeshua's question?" Stephen's words were barely audible.

"Clever! I knew Yeshua would not be beaten in argument," exclaimed Zach delightedly, having worked out the dilemma the chief priests and the others were facing. "If they say that John the Baptist's right to baptise was from heaven, how will they explain why they did not believe in him? On the other hand, if they say John's right to baptise was merely from human beings, many of the people gathered here, not to mention the many others who would hear of their reply later, would turn against them. For many, John was a prophet from God."

The priests, elders and teachers of the Law heatedly argued on and on amongst themselves. As they argued, one or two looked at Yeshua with barely-concealed hate.

"I think they have finally worked out their answer," observed Stephen, as one of the group turned to face Yeshua. It was the same man who had asked the question in the first place. He cleared his throat, and spoke in measured tones.

"We don't know," he said, as if pronouncing a verdict in court.

The three friends delightedly turned to one another. Zach noticed that James had a rare smile on his face. But Yeshua was not finished with the authorities yet. He began to tell a story.

"Once there was a man who planted a vineyard, put a fence around it, dug a hole for the wine press, and built a watch tower. Then he rented the vineyard to tenants and left home to go on a trip."

The authorities turned to one another wondering where all this was going.

"When the time came to gather the grapes, he sent a slave to the tenants to get his share of the harvest. The tenants grabbed the slave, beat him up, and sent him back without anything. Then the owner sent another slave. The tenants beat him over the head and treated him shamefully. The owner sent a third slave, and they killed him. They treated many others the same way, beating some and killing others. The only one left to send was the man's own dear son. So, last of all, he sent his son to the tenants. 'I am sure they will respect my son,' he said. But the tenants said to one another, 'This is the owner's son. Come on, let's kill him, and his property will be ours!' So they grabbed the son and killed him and threw his body out of the vineyard."

Yeshua, having finished his story, looked directly at the priests, the teachers of the Law and the elders and asked them, "What, then, will the owner of the vineyard do?"

The chief priests, teachers of the Law and the elders just stood there utterly stunned, scared at what Yeshua might say next.

"They surely know well that this story is indeed about Israel and themselves, the vineyard being Israel, and the tenants being themselves," Zach commented.

Ruth took it up. "And those who were thrashed and killed were the prophets, and the beloved son of the vineyard's owner is no doubt Yeshua himself. You told me that 'beloved son' was the title that Yeshua heard at his baptism."

"Exactly, Ruth. But what will happen now?" asked Zach.

After some nervous shuffling and mumbling one chief priest said, "We don't have to listen to all this nonsense!"

But, in case there was any lingering doubt left, Yeshua declared, "He will come and kill those tenants and turn the vineyard to others. Have you not read this scripture? 'The stone which the builders rejected as worthless turned out to be the most important of all. This was done by the Lord; what a wonderful sight it is!'"

The whole area was silent then, except for a few coughs and some shuffling of feet.

"What an end," said Ruth softly but with fear in her voice. "The tenants are wiped out, and the vineyard is given to other people. There couldn't have been a worse ending as far as the priests, the teachers of the Law and the elders of our people are concerned. They are wiped out. But so also is the 'beloved son'. What then! Is Yeshua to die too?"

CHAPTER 27

"That's unusual," mused Zach as he looked at the dress of the new arrivals, "there are both Pharisees and Herodians in this new group."

Ruth was angry as she spoke, "The last time I saw such a group together was when they were talking outside my window in Capernaum and they spoke about killing Yeshua."

"I remember that," said Stephen, "you were sick and you got out of your bed to have a look at them."

"You have a great memory, Stephen. That was three years ago," Ruth complimented him, and then looked back at the newly-arrived group who were standing near to Yeshua and his followers.

"Teacher, we know that you tell the truth, without worrying about what people think," one of them said. "You pay no attention to anyone's status, but teach the truth about God's will for all people."

"That is an ominous start," Ruth said, as she looked carefully to see if any of them belonged to the group that had passed by her window. "Beware of those who praise you, but who are really out to trick you," she warned Zach and Stephen.

"You are so right, Ruth," agreed Zach. "I think they are really saying, 'Yes, you gullible people assembled here, Yeshua is a good man but a rather limited one and not to be taken seriously. His idea of truth is very inadequate. Remember, he is just a poor nobody from Nazareth.'"

"You see, they have nothing to fear," Stephen added. "They most probably have the backing of the elders and the teachers of the Law and of ruthless King Herod himself."

A small man with a serious expression, dark eyes, a short beard and an icy 'Mount Hermon' smile, put the question to Yeshua, "Tell us, is it against our Law to pay taxes to the Emperor? Should we pay them or not?"

Zach got suddenly annoyed and only just stopped himself from using some very bad language. "That's a nasty, snake-like trap! 'Yes' puts the majority of Israel against Yeshua and 'no' will cause Yeshua to be accused of treason. How could people who are supposed to be good, indeed who pray, fast and strive for purity before God, be involved in this trickery?"

"Don't worry, Zach, Yeshua will see through it and sort it out somehow." Ruth had a certain look of confidence as she spoke, waiting for Yeshua's reply.

"Why are you trying to trap me?" Yeshua quietly answered, shaking his head.

"Look at all the people who have gathered. Everyone is waiting for Yeshua's reply." Stephen spoke under his breath.

"Bring a denarius and let me see it," Yeshua said, looking straight at the questioners.

The questioners were dumbfounded and wondered what a denarius had to do with the issue.

Zach chuckled, "Yeshua doesn't even have a denarius."

The questioners fumbled in their cloaks and one of them handed a denarius to Yeshua. Then, like hunters, they waited.

Yeshua looked carefully at the denarius as if he hardly recognised it, and then, with a half-playful smile on his face as though he were speaking to naughty children, he asked them a question, "Whose face and name are on this coin?"

His interrogators were slow to answer but before Yeshua had repeated the question they replied, "The Emperor's."

Yeshua then looked at his questioners as if he hadn't heard what they had said. They had to repeat it even louder, "The Emperor's."

Then, as if effortlessly landing a very difficult fish, Yeshua just said to them, "Then pay to the Emperor what belongs to the Emperor, and pay to God what belongs to God."

The gang let out cries of delight, but had to stifle them because some people threw them angry looks.

Then Zach became reflective and admitted, "In a way I am sorry for the Pharisees and Herodians. They probably have been put up to this. I'm sure they are normally good men who just don't understand what Yeshua is about."

"I hope," said Stephen, "that they will finally grasp the truth, that no one has a chance against Yeshua."

"I'd like to hear what John thinks of all this," said Zach.

After the questioners had left, another group arrived. They were Sadducees.

"Teacher," said one of the Sadducees, "Moses wrote this law for us: 'If a man dies and leaves a wife, but no children, that man's brother must marry the widow so that they can have children who will be considered the dead man's children.'"

Yeshua looked at the speaker but said nothing.

"Once there were seven brothers," the man continued. "The oldest got married and died without having children. Then the second one married the woman, and he also died without having any children. The same thing happened to the third brother, and then to the rest. All seven brothers married the woman and died without having children. Last of all, the woman died. Now when all the dead rise to life on the day of resurrection, whose wife will she be? All seven of them had married her."

"What a story!" said Stephen, hardly able to believe what he was hearing, "It must have taken them a long time to concoct it."

"Are the Sadducees trying to make a joke of the idea of an afterlife?" Ruth suggested as she assessed the visitors.

"They could be, Ruth," said Zach. "They don't believe in it at all."

Just then, in his deep, clear, unhesitating voice, Yeshua replied. "How wrong you are! And do you know why? It is because you don't know the Scriptures or God's power. For when the dead rise to life, they will be like the angels in heaven and will not marry. Now, as for the dead being raised; haven't you ever read in the Book of Moses the passage about the burning bush? There it is written that God said to Moses, 'I am the God of Abraham, the God of Isaac, and the God of Jacob.' He is the God of the living, not of the dead. You are completely wrong!"

Zach found it hard to hold back from laughing.

"The Sadducees must be furious! There is no comeback to what Yeshua has just said, none at all. Look, they're looking at him with badly concealed hate – what do you think, Ruth? Stephen?"

"Absolutely!" they both replied.

"They are not used to being defeated in public debate," Zach continued, "and certainly not by a 'craftsman from Galilee'. And they know that they can't buy him off."

The Sadducees turned to one another, shrugged and pretended that this was only a small setback for them.

Zach quietly said, "I think that somehow they will want to get even. I don't know how, but if they can, they will."

"Another questioner," whispered Ruth. "He was listening intently to what Yeshua was saying to the Sadducees. Do you see him? It's the elderly man with the long, white beard. He has a large face and nose... over there."

"I see him," answered Zach, trying to put aside his feeling of foreboding. "He is rather small, not easy to see. He reminds me of my grand-uncle, who was a favourite in our house. Unlike most of the others here, he seems kind."

The new questioner spoke in a soft but clear voice, "Which commandment is the most important of all?"

Yeshua looked at the man and, showing deep respect, answered him, "The most important one is this: 'Listen, Israel! The Lord our God is the only Lord. Love the Lord your God with all your heart, with all your soul, with all your mind and with all your strength.' The second most important commandment is this: 'Love your neighbour as you love yourself.' There are no other commandments more important than these two."

The teacher of the Law smiled with a great joy that lit up his face. He said to Yeshua, "Well done, Teacher! It is true, as you say, that only the Lord is God and that there is no other god but Him. And you must love God with all your strength; and you must love your neighbour as you love yourself. It is more important to obey these two commandments than to offer animals on the altar and other sacrifices to God."

Yeshua looked at the elderly teacher of the Law and with deep admiration said, "You are not far from the kingdom of God."

The teacher smiled again at Yeshua, bowed politely and walked slowly and happily away.

"I think," said Zach, "that that teacher is very lucky. Firstly, he believes in God. Secondly, his views have been affirmed by Yeshua and thirdly and most important of all, he is 'not far from the kingdom of God.'"

"Zach, I think you are beginning to believe in the God of Yeshua and maybe you too are not far from the kingdom of God." Ruth looked straight into Zach's eyes.

Zach smiled at her. "If only," he replied.

Chapter 28

Later that afternoon, they returned to the Temple and Yeshua was still there surrounded by a crowd of people. He was sitting on the steps and talking to them.

"Yeshua is contradicting the interpretation of the teachers of the Law," said Ruth, very worried. "What will they do if he continues to confront them?"

Zach and Stephen were wondering the same thing.

"Watch out for the teachers of the Law," continued Yeshua, "who like to walk around in their long robes and be greeted with respect in the marketplace; who choose the reserved seats in the synagogues and the best places at feasts. They take advantage of widows and rob them of their homes, and then make a show of saying long prayers. Their punishment will be all the worse."

After this second attack on the teachers of the Law, Zach murmured, "If I didn't believe Yeshua was able to deal with these people, I would be very uneasy now."

Shortly, Yeshua indicated that he would continue the teaching at another time. After he had spoken to a few who had problems and had lingered behind, the crowd was gone. Many of the Twelve had also left to help arrange for the coming feast, but John, James, Peter and Andrew remained. Yeshua turned towards the gang and, looking at them with a broad smile, he motioned them to join him.

"Look, Ruth and Stephen," said Zach, utterly delighted, "Yeshua is calling us."

"Let's go," said Stephen, as if he feared losing a moment of this precious time.

Yeshua greeted them and began walking towards the steps that led from the women's court to the men's section of the Court of Israel.

As they did so, Zach had a word with John. "John, who gets the money that goes into those trumpet-like money chests over there?" He pointed to a number of chests into which people were dropping money.

"As I explained before, Zach, it is very, very expensive to run Jerusalem. From the High Priest down to the gate-keepers, there are many hundreds of people involved in keeping the Temple functioning. It is not merely prayer and sacrifices that take place here. Day by day there is a great deal of maintenance – cleaning, mending, painting and indeed guarding all the sacred vessels and ritual garments... and much more. Whether we like it or not, money is very much part of it all. It has to be if the Temple is to be kept as beautiful as it is and made to function properly. Remember, it is God's house of prayer."

By the time John had finished explaining the ins and outs of running the Temple, the whole group had reached the steps and were slowly climbing them so as to have a better view of the court below and especially 'the treasury' – the trumpet-shaped containers for voluntary offerings of money. After a few steps Yeshua sat down and everyone else followed suit.

Ruth was right beside a smiling Yeshua, while Stephen, Zach and the other four sat just below them, two steps down.

At first they all just watched in silence. A large number of people were putting coins into the money chests. "Some of these people are very rich," Zach remarked.

"It's good they are giving money for the upkeep of the Temple," John said.

Just then Yeshua quietly pointed out an old woman who was very stooped and shuffling very slowly towards one of the chests.

"She is a great age," observed Ruth. "Her fingers are bent and the poor woman seems to have difficulty opening the little piece of cloth with her money in it."

At last, having taken out her money, the old woman stretched out her frail arm and put coins into the chest.

Ruth said with great sadness, "She has only put in two leptons. She came all this way to put in two leptons?"

They watched as the old woman rolled up her little piece of cloth, and then moved away slowly. As she began to leave, Yeshua turned to the gang and said, "I tell you that this poor widow has put more in the offering box than all the others. For the others put in what they had to spare of their riches, but she, poor as she is, gave away all she had to live on."

"Yeshua, is that the way God looks at life?" asked Zach.

It wasn't really a question but a statement. Seeing Yeshua's smile, Zach recognised that Yeshua was teaching them the way God thinks.

As the group reached the side of the Temple, Andrew, Peter's brother, said to Yeshua, "Look, Teacher! What wonderful stones and buildings!"

But Yeshua looked at him with what seemed like sadness, and replying said, "You see these great buildings? Not a single stone here will be left in its place. Every one of them will be thrown down."

Ruth asked Zach anxiously, "Did you hear that?"

"Yes I did, Ruth, but didn't Yeshua already say much the same thing when we were entering Jerusalem... and nothing has happened?" But Zach knew that this time Yeshua's remark had struck Ruth more forcibly than it had before.

"Yeshua is, has always been, and will always be, in complete control," he continued. "There is no need to worry. And anyway, he's sure to look after the person who sat right beside him watching the people donating to the Treasury." Ruth laughed a little but Zach knew that she was still worried.

The young friends, having left the Temple area, went to Zebedee's shop and adjoining house, to be with the other pilgrims. Meanwhile, Yeshua and the four members of his Twelve went to the Mount of Olives.

Chapter 29

"Can you believe it, there are only two days left before the Passover feast and the Feast of Unleavened Bread?" Salome was chatting with Zach. "Yes, this wonderful double feast rekindles so many memories of God's kindness to our people. After the seven days of the feast we will all be very tired."

"We will," agreed Zach. "Mum, is there anything I can do for you?"

"Not at all, Zach, go quickly. I know Ruth is to meet you after her short visit to the Temple. She loved being with Yeshua yesterday." Salome looked at him affectionately as she began preparing some food. "Off with you," she said.

Zach gave her a hug and left. He met Stephen coming down the stairs and they set off. Then they saw Ruth walking fast down the street towards them. She seemed excited but also in some way upset.

"Is there something wrong, Ruth?" asked Zach.

Ruth explained, "I was up at the Temple area because I wanted to have another look at the court where we were yesterday... and, well, I heard it again."

"Heard what?" asked Zach, his concern mounting.

"Do you remember when I was sick in Capernaum and I heard some Pharisees and Herodians saying that they were looking for a chance to kill Yeshua?"

"How could we forget?" Zach and Stephen spoke in unison.

"Well, when I was in the court this morning watching all the people putting money into the chests, a small group of well-dressed Pharisees and teachers of the Law, with some Herodians, were muttering together rather suspiciously, at least that's what I thought. So, I moved nearer to the group to see if I could hear anything. I pretended to be looking at the buildings. The long-robed people speaking in Greek probably thought that a country person like me wouldn't be able to understand them. At one stage, as I got nearer, one of them focused his eyes on me and told me in Greek to move away, but I looked at him as if I didn't understand and just smiled back and said 'Thank you' in our own language. He continued to stare at me but then just shrugged his shoulders and turned back to the group. Well, they were discussing how to capture Yeshua and then quietly have him killed without it being noticed."

"Are you sure, Ruth?" asked Zach.

"Certain!" said Ruth. "And they mentioned something about the Romans. Unfortunately, I could only stay for a few minutes, in case they became suspicious. One of them, an older one, said, 'We must not do it during the festival or the people might riot.' That was the last thing I heard. It's not good news." Ruth looked carefully at Zach and Stephen to see how they felt about this new turn of events.

Zach tried to sound positive, even though he was deeply upset. "What's new?" he said, "We've always known that they are unhappy with Yeshua. They may threaten but nothing will happen."

"All the same, Zach, I think we should tell John to pass on this information to Yeshua," Stephen said.

As luck would have it, John was coming towards them with James and two others. Zach called John aside. John listened to Ruth's story with complete attention and then said, "We are aware of the negative things that are being talked about here in Jerusalem. James and I have friends who keep us fully up-to-date. But you know well that Yeshua can deal with all problems, no matter how difficult. Have you not seen how he has defeated the authorities in every argument already? No, they are no match for him." John smiled and rejoined James and his friends.

"You see, Ruth, John is right. Yeshua is unafraid, so why should we be?" Zach put his arm around Ruth's shoulder as he spoke and they began walking up the town. "We will of course keep an eye out and stay close to him as much as we can, so that we can warn him if we see something, something that he mightn't be expecting. Although as far as I can see Yeshua always seems to be fully aware of what's happening around him."

<hr>

138

That evening, Yeshua was invited to a house in Bethany owned by 'Simon the Leper', whom he had previously cured of leprosy. Simon lived very near to a friend of Yeshua's called Lazarus, who lived with his sisters Mary and Martha.

That evening, at Simon's house, there was a fairly large group of people sitting down at table, including the Twelve. They were mostly business people, many of whom were visiting Jerusalem for the feast. The gang were also invited to attend since they also knew the family. When the meal was under way, Mary, Lazarus's sister, came in carrying a jar of very precious ointment.

"Mary is a really beautiful woman," observed Stephen.

Mary had long dark hair, dark brown eyes and a most attractive personality. "She always dresses with great care and carries herself with the grace of a queen," said Ruth.

"What is she doing now?" asked Stephen, noticing that she had gone over to Yeshua and, without saying a word, had begun pouring ointment on his head, and he was not telling her to stop. In fact, he seemed quite content with what was happening.

"I have smelled that same ointment on some very rich people. I think it is very expensive," said Stephen admiringly, "and I think she is going to use up the whole jar, judging by the way she is pouring it on."

Mary did indeed continue to pour on the ointment until the jar was empty.

"Listen," said Zach, "to those murmurs of disapproval. I think they are coming from the Twelve."

"You're right, Zach," said Stephen sounding amazed.

Then one of the Twelve spoke. It was Judas.

"What is the use of wasting perfume?" Judas said, addressing Mary.

"I don't believe it," whispered Ruth, "how can he say that?"

"It could have been sold for over three hundred denarii," Judas continued accusingly, "and the money given to the poor."

"You know, Ruth, I believe that Judas, though speaking to Mary, is really complaining to Yeshua," confided Zach.

"Three hundred denarii is equivalent to almost a year's payment for a worker," Stephen quietly announced. "If it hadn't been poured on Yeshua's head, it would have gone to waste."

Ruth gave Stephen a stern look of disapproval.

Then Yeshua came to Mary's aid. "Leave her alone!" he said. "Why are you bothering her? She has done a fine and beautiful thing for me. You will always have poor people with you and, any time you want to, you can help them. But you will not always have me. She did what she could. She poured ointment on my body to prepare it ahead of time for burial."

Judas on hearing the words 'you will not always have me' and then 'burial', was shocked. So was everyone else present.

"If this anointing was really for his burial, it means that his death must be very near," Ruth said as she turned to Zach and Stephen.

Then Yeshua, looking at everyone in the room, said, "Now, I assure you that wherever the good news is preached all over the world, what she has done will be told in memory of her."

"Listen to that!" said Stephen, "Yeshua obviously sees a worldwide future for his teaching and his loving way of life. Isn't that wonderful?"

Zach said nothing, but thought to himself, 'Stephen has a point. But if Yeshua is about to die very soon, are we the ones appointed to pass on his teaching? Will he really die soon, really die?'

As the three sat there at the meal it sank in that the authorities in Jerusalem must really be out to get Yeshua and kill him.

'And Judas? Why was he so negative?' Stephen silently wondered.

It was only days later that the gang heard what had happened next. They had thought they had a good idea of what was going on but, in fact, they really didn't know how far things had actually gone.

CHAPTER 30

"What will you give me if I betray Yeshua of Nazareth to you?" Judas spoke with confidence to impress the chief priests and some Temple guards who were standing in the shadow of the Temple.

"I didn't expect this windfall," murmured the most senior chief priest to a colleague standing beside him.

"We could possibly stretch to thirty pieces of silver?" The man who said this looked quickly at his colleague who indicated agreement. So the chief priest smiled at Judas and said, "I hope thirty pieces of silver is enough?" Then he slowly counted out thirty pieces of silver and put them in a small pouch. Judas did not stop him or argue. The chief priest then offered the full pouch to Judas.

Judas couldn't believe how much they were willing to give, but he pretended to be quite unimpressed. 'They really must want Yeshua very badly,' he thought to himself. But when it was offered he put out his hand and took the pouch grudgingly, as though it was barely enough. Smiling politely Judas then left them in the shadows with the assurance that he would look for the right time to hand Yeshua over to them. The chief priests smiled triumphantly as he left.

Weeks later, when Zach looked back at what had happened during those days, he felt that someone should have noticed what Judas was up to. But the truth was that no one seemed to have had any idea at all. The gang did ask themselves whether Yeshua himself knew about Judas. Ruth believed that he did. She said that there was no doubt but that Yeshua knew, since he was aware of everything.

'If Ruth is right,' thought Zach, 'then it is very hard to understand why Yeshua did nothing to stop him.'

"I wonder where we will go to celebrate the Passover meal," said Stephen voicing his concern. "I suppose that we will probably be split up."

Zach smiled and said, "My mother has just informed me that we are all going to celebrate together at her cousin's house."

"Will Yeshua and the Twelve be there?" asked Ruth with excitement.

"I believe so," said Zach, smiling broadly. "Yeshua wouldn't celebrate it without you being there, Ruth."

Ruth smiled and shook her head. Stephen laughed.

"We have laughed so little since we have come to Jerusalem," said Zach somewhat despondently.

Zach began to sing, and Stephen joined in, and in no time the three were singing together.

That morning they helped with various chores around the house and, after a rest in the middle of the day, got themselves ready for the evening meal and helped the women prepare some of the food, while trying not to get in their way.

"I presume Peter and John have gone to remove all the leavened food from the house where the meal will take place," said Zach. "The layout of the room is also important because particular places will need to be arranged with Yeshua's position as 'Father of the Family' at the centre of everything."

"The lamb, too, has to be prepared for the occasion, so Peter and John have much to do," added Ruth, as she counted various items on special dishes.

"This house is very near the South Wall," Zach said, as he worked out his bearings. "If we hadn't been here for some days already, it would have been fairly difficult to follow the directions given to us."

"Finding our way through the huge number of visitors was difficult, but keeping our eyes on the houses and palaces made it fairly easy," said Ruth.

"Yes, there are thousands of visitors in the city. But did you ever see so many sheep, hundreds and hundreds of them?" asked Stephen.

"Never," said Ruth.

As the three stood in front of the house where the Passover meal would take place, Zach spoke seriously, "Ruth and Stephen," Zach said, "I doubt if we will ever forget this meal. To share a Passover meal with Yeshua is such a huge gift for us."

Zach began looking at the house and working out its position in relation to the High Priest's house and Pilate's palace, a little further away.

"We are in good company," continued Zach, who turned to enter the house. As they entered Stephen noticed the upstairs area.

"Look at all the couches upstairs. Salome, will the meal be held up there?" Stephen asked. She, along with the other women, had been in the house for some time already.

"Yes, Stephen. Let me show you your three places for the meal," Salome replied, rubbing her hands on a cloth as she led them up the wooden stairs.

"These places here are for the Twelve and those ones over there, near the service tables, are for the three of you. You will be able to help us serve from there and at the same time hear most of the conversation. Oh yes! This is John Mark." A young boy of around eight years of age appeared. "John Mark is the son of my first cousin who owns this house... John Mark, this is my son Zach, whom I was telling you about, and these are his two friends, Ruth and Stephen."

"Great to meet you, John Mark," said Zach as they all greeted him.

"You have a beautiful house here," said Ruth admiringly.

"Yes, I suppose we have. My dad works for Caiaphas, the High Priest, and Annas, his father." John Mark smiled but was a little overawed by all the visitors whom he had never met before.

"I must get back to my study-room," continued John Mark politely, "my dad gives me some study to do everyday."

"You are very fortunate, John Mark," Zach said, looking at him encouragingly. "Keep it up, even if sometimes it might be more fun to be out playing with your friends."

"I will," replied John Mark, with a shy smile. Then he disappeared into an adjoining room.

"Look, Zach!" said Ruth. "We have a view through this window of the High Priest's house. Goodness, look at all the lights around it. They weren't alight when we arrived."

Zach and Stephen looked out the window and saw what Ruth was talking about. The palace looked magnificent.

"Caiaphas is certainly a very important person in Israel," said Stephen.

"He certainly is..." agreed Zach. "Let's go down and offer our help with the meal."

When they arrived downstairs they were given instructions on a number of jobs that they could do – bringing food, clearing and replacing food on the table and making sure that there was water for hand washing.

"Who put the towel and basin there for washing feet?" asked Zach.

"It was John," replied Salome, as she gave various instructions regarding the meal to the women who were around her, including Ruth. "It is, as you know Zach, a tradition in Galilee to wash feet, but John felt, on this occasion, that we would practise it here too in Judah."

Zach said nothing but all of a sudden he felt very hungry as he looked at some of the dishes that would be presented.

Then a great rushing to and fro began. "I think Yeshua and the Twelve must be here," said Ruth as she stopped and looked at the entrance hall.

The Twelve all seemed fairly serious as they came in, but probably they were a little tired. Yeshua, on the other hand, seemed fit and well, and told everyone that he had been looking forward to this meal for some time.

"Zach, will you show Yeshua and the Twelve to their places?" Salome asked with a smile.

"Sure, Mum," he replied, and then led them up the stairs and pointed to their places. In a short time they were all sitting down. But just then everyone went silent.

"Look at that!" said Zach with amazement.

Yeshua had taken off his outer garment and had taken the bowl and towel, left there by John, and was preparing to wash the feet of the Twelve.

Everyone was lost for words.

"But servants are supposed to do that," said Stephen with a bewildered frown.

"I know," said Zach, barely audibly.

"You are not going to wash my feet, Lord," said Peter to Yeshua. He was having none of it. But Yeshua looked into his eyes and quietly said, "You do not understand now what I am doing, but you will understand later."

Peter, shocked, looked at Yeshua and protested, his voice becoming hoarse, "Never at any time will you wash my feet!"

Yeshua was unfazed and said, "If I do not wash your feet, you will no longer be my disciple."

"Peter can't win," said Zach.

"Not only my feet, but also my hands and head!" said Peter.

Yeshua smiled and began washing Peter's feet.

"It's really all or nothing for Peter," murmured Zach, enthralled. "This surely makes it clear that Yeshua will do anything for the Twelve and indeed for all of us, regardless of our unworthiness and the stupidity of our lives."

"He has often said 'I have come to call sinners!'" added Ruth.

In silence they watched Yeshua carefully wash the feet of all the Twelve. Then, when he had finished, he put his outer garment back on and sat down in his place between John and Judas, at the centre of the table.

Chapter 31

"When Yeshua had finished washing the feet of the Twelve they all stood in silence," Zach was telling his two sisters and his father, Zebedee, some weeks later. "And then Yeshua prayed the ritual prayer of sanctification which mentions our deliverance from Egypt. After that, the pouring of the First Cup was performed and another short prayer was said. Then they all drank the First Cup and began eating.

Next, Yeshua dipped a bitter herb in the salty water together with John who was sitting beside him. The herbs were passed on to the rest of the group who also dipped them in the water. It could have been vinegar but on that night it was salty water. Then, after the bitter herbs were eaten and Stephen, Ruth and I were removing all the food from the table, Yeshua said, 'I tell you that one of you will betray me – one who is eating with me.'

That brought a new meaning to the word bitter. We were all really upset when Yeshua said that. Indeed, John was almost in tears. They all protested strongly, particularly Peter.

But it was time to pour the Second Cup, so Stephen, Ruth and I acted as waiters.

However, Peter's upset about the betrayal would not go away, so he leaned over to John who was sitting between Peter and Yeshua and asked him to ask Yeshua who it was who was going to betray him. So John leant over to Yeshua and whispered, 'Who is it, Lord?'

Yeshua very quietly answered him, 'I will dip some bread in the sauce and give it to him; he is the man,' and Yeshua dipped the bread in the sauce and gave it to Judas.

At the time I didn't hear this bit of the conversation but John filled me in later. You might think that John and Peter would be shocked, but they weren't."

"Why not Zach?" asked Elizabeth, removing her hand from under her chin as she lay on the floor listening to every word.

"I think, Elizabeth," answered Zach, "that when they heard the answer from Yeshua they just didn't understand. Either that or they just couldn't believe that Judas could be involved in a betrayal."

"I find it hard to believe, too," murmured Zebedee.

"Sometime later, John told me that Yeshua, with tears in his eyes, had told him quietly at the meal that it would have been better for the man who was to betray him if he had never been born. When John told me this, for some reason I was sure that Yeshua would forgive Judas. What Yeshua had foretold, I think, was that Judas' actual dying would be awful.

"After awhile, Judas said he had to leave to attend to some matter. When he had gone Yeshua began to talk about love, and that giving one's life for others was true love, and his commandment for us was that we should love one another as he, Yeshua, had loved us. At the time, I thought that this was too much to ask of us since his love was so great that our love could not compare with his in any way, and little did I know to what lengths his love would go.

"Then after the delicious meal, to our surprise, Yeshua took up the last of the unleavened bread and blessed it and broke it. He passed the broken bread around and said, 'Take it, this is my body which is given for you. Do this in memory of me.'

"Well, we had just celebrated in symbols the memorial of our escape from Egypt by the power of God. Now Yeshua was asking us to take the broken bread that was his body... What could that mean? Then it hit me. His death must be going to happen very, very soon. Ruth, on hearing what Yeshua said, became quite emotional while Stephen just stared, past those seated in front of him, at Yeshua and murmured, 'This unleavened bread is his body? Given for us?'"

"That was very strange, Zach," Elizabeth said – her eyes were beginning to be tired.

"But that wasn't the end of it," continued Zach. "After reciting the normal prayer of the Passover ritual which is 'I will redeem you with outstretched arm and with great judgment,' and which is said just before the Third Cup is drunk, Yeshua said to all of us, as he held the Cup, 'This is my blood which is poured out for all, my blood which seals God's covenant.'

"That was the final blow for me and my friends and I think for almost everyone in the room. We couldn't misunderstand that. He was surely going to die a bloody death and somehow, in some mysterious way, this wine was his blood."

Zach continued, "The Eleven — Judas, you remember, was no longer there — indeed all of us, were slow to drink the wine, and when we did, it was with a kind of deep wonder and reverence.

"Ruth asked me what was happening but I had no answer. Stephen, now convinced, said, 'This is dreadful. Something truly terrible is going to happen... We will certainly remember this night, the bread, his body, and the wine, his blood.'

"I just hoped that somehow things would be different, and that Yeshua would be alright.

"The Fourth Cup was then poured and drunk and Yeshua explained in words that, again, could not be misunderstood, 'I tell you, I will never again drink this wine until the day I drink new wine in the Kingdom of God.'

Yes, we were absolutely certain then that this was the beginning of the end. We could no longer doubt it. Terrible things were to happen. Yeshua had warned us all along that they would."

"It's time for you two girls to go to bed," said Zebedee. The two girls looked at their dad, but knew that his word was law.

"All right, Dad! Thanks, Zach," said Esther, kissing him goodnight. Elizabeth, just three years older, stood up, stretched herself, rubbed her eyes and then smiled at Zach. "But, Zach, Yeshua won in the end, didn't he?"

Zach, barely holding back his tears, replied, "Of course he did, Elizabeth, of course he did." Elizabeth reached up and put her arms around his neck and hugged him. He felt that she understood how sad he was.

CHAPTER 32

The meal was over, all involved in preparing it had been thanked and now the gang walked behind the Eleven on the way to the lower city and home.

"It's a joy to be with Yeshua, but how long will it last... when will his death happen?" Zach found himself looking at the lights of the High Priest's house as he spoke.

"I still don't fully believe that Yeshua will die," Ruth said, trying to instil optimism. But Zach knew by her voice that she too was miserable.

For the next few minutes they walked along in silence listening to the sounds of the city. The Eleven were talking among themselves nearby. Yeshua was silent for a time. Then he spoke.

"All of you will run away and leave me," he said, "for the scripture says, 'God will kill the shepherd, and the sheep will all be scattered.' But after I am raised to life, I will go into Galilee ahead of you."

"Did you hear that, Zach?" asked Stephen in an anxious whisper.

"I did," said Zach but he was waiting for the response of the Eleven.

"I will never leave you, even though all the rest do!" It was Peter, and he was definitely not going to accept what Yeshua had said.

"There is no doubt but that Peter really loves Yeshua," said Ruth warmly. Yeshua just then put his arm around Peter's shoulder and spelt out for him what would happen.

"Peter, I tell you that before the cock crows two times tonight, you will say three times that you do not know me."

But Peter was having none of it. It just couldn't be true. He took two steps forward and turned to Yeshua and looking him straight in the eyes announced, "I will never say that, even if I have to die with you."

The others, who were listening intently, echoed this. "No, we feel the same as Peter. None of us will disown you."

But Yeshua just looked at them and slowly and sadly shook his head.

At that point the group had reached Zebedee's house in the Lower City, near to the gate, and Salome, who had arrived a little earlier, offered Yeshua a private room there for the night, which he declined. He thanked her, but said that he would rather go to Zebedee's olive garden with the Eleven and sleep there in the open.

When Yeshua left with the Eleven, Zach, Stephen and Ruth wanted to go to the olive garden too. Zach pleaded, "Mum, we can sleep in the little house in the garden. The caretaker only sleeps in one room. There are two other rooms. We'll be fine."

Salome did not reject the idea out of hand but went in to consult the other women and in a few minutes returned. "You may go, but I am going too. Ruth and I will take one room and you, Zach and Stephen, can use the other."

Soon the three friends and Salome were hurrying to the house in the olive garden of Gethsemane. Salome had not told them why she agreed to allow them to go there, but it was because she wanted to watch out not merely for one of her sons, Zach, but for all three sons. She didn't want anything to happen to James or John either.

Salome and Ruth walked together, as did Stephen and Zach. "Zach, what did you make of the idea of Peter denying Yeshua 'before the cock crows two times'? Could Yeshua have been talking about the trumpet blasts at the end of the third watch?" asked Stephen.

"That's exactly what I think, Stephen. The trumpeters sound twice, in different directions, during great feasts since there are so many people in the city."

"Do you think that whatever's going to happen might happen tonight, Zach?"

Zach looked at Stephen, "I hope not, but, yes, I do think it could be tonight."

"An old guard lives on his own in one of the rooms," Salome was explaining to Ruth as they crossed the bridge and began walking along the valley of the Kidron. "The other two rooms are fairly large and my husband and I made sure that they were good enough to have visitors stay there. I think we'll sleep well."

"I doubt if Zach will sleep, Salome, he is very frightened for Yeshua," Ruth said. "He pretends that he is not, but I know he is. If anything happened to Yeshua, Zach would be in a terrible state."

'Ruth is so mature,' Salome thought. Then she quietly said, "Ruth, you are perfectly right, you know him well... here we are... and look over there. Yeshua and the Eleven have only arrived just ahead of us."

"Mum, can Stephen and I sleep in the open? We've become quite used to it over the past three years," Zach said, aware that he was pushing it.

"Zach, maybe another night, but not tonight... you really need a good sleep."

Zach expected that reply, and there was no use arguing, but 'it was worth a try,' he said to himself. So he and Stephen began organising themselves in their room. "Do you think you will sleep, Zach?" asked Stephen yawning.

"I hope to, I do feel quite tired. You seem to be too," Zach replied.

"I am nearly asleep already." Stephen was fast asleep before Zach had even got into bed.

It was a fairly warm night and Yeshua and the Eleven were happy just to find a suitable place in the olive grove and rest there. Yeshua, however, was not going to settle down and sleep without prayer. Despite all the prayers and hymns said and sung during the Passover meal, Yeshua said to the Eleven, as they began to make themselves comfortable, "Sit here while I pray."

Yeshua then asked Peter, James and John to go with him a little further into the garden to look for a more private spot.

"Yeshua is really distressed, James," whispered John as they followed Yeshua. "I have seen him agitated before but never like tonight," James agreed.

"The sorrow in my heart is so great that it almost crushes me," Yeshua said to them, hardly able to look into their eyes. "Stay here and keep watch."

James and John exchanged looks. They were certainly going to stay awake. And Peter, who was still troubled by Yeshua telling him that he would deny him three times, would most definitely stay awake.

"Certainly, Yeshua," they said, even though they were exhausted.

Yeshua went on alone a little further into the garden. Arriving at the place where he chose to pray, he threw himself on the ground and began to pray. "Abba, everything is possible for you. Take this cup of suffering away from me. Yet not what I want, but what you want."

Yeshua slowly said this over and over again. After an hour of prayer, Yeshua returned to the three Apostles... they were fast asleep.

"It was weakness and laziness," John later confided sadly to his family, "at what was to be a most decisive moment in Yeshua's life. Yes, we were asleep despite all our promises. And Yeshua needed our support, especially that night."

When they suddenly awoke they saw Yeshua standing in front of them. He was distraught. His hair bedraggled, he was covered in sweat and his eyes seemed blood-shot. His beard had some small twigs in it, obviously picked up from the ground where he had prostrated himself in prayer.

"Simon, are you asleep?" Yeshua asked quietly, raising his eyebrows a little. "Weren't you able to stay awake for even one hour?"

'He called him Simon and not Peter, the 'Rock',' John noted to himself.

Simon Peter was so annoyed with himself, so terribly annoyed with himself, that the two Zebedee brothers felt really sorry for him. But James and John realised that they were just as guilty. Yeshua looked at them with what they felt was a kind of loving sadness in his eyes, like a worried but forgiving parent.

"The spirit is willing but the flesh is weak," he said.

Then Yeshua, once again, quietly walked back to where he had been and again threw himself down on the ground and continued his prayer with the same words as before, "Abba, everything is possible for you. Take this cup of suffering away from me. Yet not what I want, but what you want."

John, seeing Yeshua go back to where he had prayed before, propped himself up against a boulder. It was most uncomfortable but it would keep him awake. James, too, sat up with his back straight, leaning most uncomfortably against an olive tree. Meanwhile, Peter walked about for a while but then went to another olive tree some paces away from where

James was, and knelt down with his arms held up by the branches of the tree. He looked, and was, extremely uncomfortable – but this time he would be awake when Yeshua returned.

Indeed, they managed to stay awake for the first half-hour waiting for Yeshua to finish, but shortly after this they again all lapsed into sleep and never heard him coming back.

Yeshua did not wake them this time but once again went back to his place of prayer and continued praying. It was only on reflection that John, semi-conscious, vaguely remembered his return.

Finally, after a third period of prayer, Yeshua returned once more. This time he did waken them. They were truly ashamed of themselves and this was made worse by seeing the state Yeshua was in. Among other things they noticed some dark sweat marks on his clothes that later, in the light, turned out to be stains of blood – Yeshua had been sweating blood.

"Are you still sleeping and resting? Enough!" Yeshua said, his voice wasn't harsh but there was urgency in it when he said 'enough'.

Hearing this and knowing that he would normally not have woken them, Peter, James and John looked around to see what the urgency was. They saw nothing.

"What's happening?" John asked James.

"I don't know," James replied.

Meanwhile, Peter, though he had very sore arms from the way he had slept, still looked for his sword. Then Yeshua spoke, simply and factually, "The hour has come! Look, the 'Son of Man' is now being handed over to the power of sinners. Get up, let us go. Look, here is the man who is betraying me."

Well, if ever there was a wake-up call that was it! The three looked at the road leading to the garden and to their complete dismay they saw the 'sinners'. A large group of people with lights was coming along the road near to the garden, with one man in front leading them. The rest of the Eleven had also woken up and they too were standing and staring at the approaching mob. It looked ominous in the extreme.

Zach and Stephen, inside the house, were also woken up by the noise of the approaching crowd. They looked anxiously out the window.

"This is really frightening, Zach." said Stephen as he held back a curtain, trying to see where the noise was coming from.

"I have never seen the Twelve so terrified. Yeshua seems to be waiting for the crowd, whoever they are," said Zach.

"Not Twelve, Zach. Eleven," Stephen reminded a tired Zach.

Just then a man came through the gate and went on past the house into the garden. He was leading a group of men who were carrying clubs and swords.

"Who are they?" murmured Stephen with great anxiety.

At that stage Ruth came running in with Salome and said, "Look, that man who just came in is Judas."

"What?" Zach said in disbelief. "Where is he? I can't see him. Yes... I see him now... it is Judas!"

"What is he doing here?" asked Stephen, peering though the window.

"I am afraid this looks very bad," Salome said slowly. Yeshua was now surrounded by the mob wielding their clubs and swords.

"They are a terrible-looking mob," said Ruth, looking out the window along with the two boys, while Salome just peered around the curtain from the side.

"I have actually seen one of those people in the Temple area earlier in the week," said Zach. "He seemed really tough."

Just then, Judas, without too much hesitation, went forward and said to Yeshua, "Teacher!"

And then he kissed Yeshua.

"Did you see that, Zach?" asked Ruth, in a state of utter confusion.

Stephen looked somewhat cheered, and with some hope in his eyes said, "Maybe it is all right after all. Maybe Judas has organised a group to make sure that Yeshua will not be killed by the leaders of the people as we all had feared. Yes, that's it!"

"Stephen, I think you're right," agreed Ruth hopefully. "Judas has probably sorted it all out."

Zach was not so sure and kept stonily silent. He remembered how Judas complained to Mary, the sister of Lazarus – 'What was the use of wasting the perfume?' as she was pouring it on Yeshua's head.

"No!" Zach cried loudly. "Look! The men with the clubs and swords are seizing Yeshua and tying him up... and Judas is not stopping them... and the Eleven are doing nothing either!" Zach looked disgusted.

"Peter is beginning to fight," said Stephen. "He seems to have hit and injured the ear of one of the mob with his sword."

"And... Yeshua is telling Peter to put the sword away," gasped Zach, with a voice that was barely audible.

"Look!" he continued. "Yeshua seems to have cured the ear of the man whom Peter struck."

Zach slipped quietly away from the others then and they assumed that he was going to relieve himself. Salome took his place, deciding to get a better look at what was happening.

"Who is that?" asked Ruth, seeing a person in a linen cloth making his way through the olive trees towards Yeshua.

"Oh no!" Salome let out a cry. "It's Zach!"

Then one of the men armed with a club saw Zach and went over to him and ripped off his garment. Zach was now left naked. The man was about to hit him but Zach ran up a path and disappeared – he had known every inch of the garden since he was a child.

"We must all leave!" Salome urged them. "Zach will be okay. That mob will take Yeshua to the Temple or to the High Priest's house. We can go back the other way. Quickly, let's get out of here."

When Salome arrived back at the house with Ruth and Stephen, there was Zach, badly out of breath. He was wearing another garment.

"It's true, Yeshua was right," Zach said, tears flowing down his face.

"What is true, Zach?" asked Ruth going over to him, putting a hand on each shoulder and looking into his streaming eyes.

"What Yeshua said would happen, has happened. All the Eleven have run away." Zach sobbed, almost inconsolably.

"What about John and James?" Salome asked, worry etched on her face.

Zach nodded his head, "I think they ran too..."

Salome was in a state of shock and went to lie down in her room. Zach started sobbing uncontrollably.

"My world has disappeared and I feel helpless, Ruth," Zach confessed to her. "If I saw those soldiers now I would curse them, and that includes our leaders who I know are behind all this. You yourself heard them plotting, Ruth."

Then the door of the house opened.

CHAPTER 33

"James, John, where have you been?" cried Zach, as he stood up, and wiped the tears from his eyes. He had a thousand questions running through his head.

John answered quickly, "James and I are going to the High Priest's house. We've found out that that's where the trouble is coming from."

James added, "We recognised a number of the High Priest's guards in the olive garden."

"How will you get in there?" asked Zach doubtfully.

"Joseph, our friend from Arimathea, has arranged it. We have met Caiaphas the High Priest a few times with him," John said as he put on his sandals. "As you can see, we are dressing for the occasion."

"Peter is following the mob," continued James, "so he can keep in touch with what's happening... we must go."

As they were about to go out the door, Salome came into the hallway with Esther and Sarah, the mothers of Ruth and Stephen.

"God go with you," Salome said to James and John. The two stopped and went over to their mother to hug her. Then, nodding to the others, they were gone.

Salome turned to the gang, "We realise that you, Zach and Stephen, will probably want to find out more about Yeshua. Sarah and I have reluctantly agreed to let you go and see if anything can be done, but you must take great care."

Then Esther looked at her daughter, "Ruth," she said, "we have discussed your case and we all feel that it would be better if you remain here in the house with us for the time being. We will join Zach and Stephen in due course."

Ruth looked at her mother and then at Salome, "But... all right," she said with a disappointed look and then a sigh of acceptance. And turning to Zach and Stephen she said, "I'll join you later – stay safe."   .

The boys quickly hurried away.

"I hope John and James are right about where we should go," said Zach as he ran along beside Stephen. "I'm not surprised that it was Caiaphas who organised all this. No doubt the Sanhedrin is already in the High Priest's house, waiting for Yeshua to be brought in. Judas probably went to Caiaphas immediately after he had left the Passover supper."

By the time they arrived at the High Priest's House, they were fairly out of breath. "Judging from the noise we're at the right place," said Stephen, "but what do we do now?" They had hidden behind the right pillar of the large ornamental gates at the entrance to the outer courtyard.

"There are quite a number of people in there around a fire," said Zach as he looked past the gate. "Look Stephen, I don't think they will notice us if we walk slowly through the gate – and when we get that far we'll look for the safest place to go."

Stephen nodded and they began walking into the courtyard as if they belonged there. Nobody stopped them. The guards were chatting together about the sudden coldness of the night, and the people at the fire were too busy keeping themselves warm.

"Stephen," whispered Zach, barely opening his mouth, "we'll go over there to the pillar beside the steps. They seem to lead to the inner courts. When we get there we'll decide what to do."

They walked slowly towards the pillars, trying not to look left or right in case they were recognised as strangers.

"What if they notice us and stop us... what then?" Stephen mouthed. They were still about ten paces away from the pillars.

"Don't worry," Zach reassured him. "We'll face any problems when they happen... we'll be all right."

They were lucky. Sitting down quietly, almost behind the pillars, they found that nobody was worried about them and at the same time they were quite near to where all the noise was coming from.

"I think we'll wait here, Stephen," said Zach, summing up the situation. "It could be dangerous to go any further. This doorway seems to be the main way for leaving the house, and so we'll be able to see Yeshua when whatever is happening inside is over."

"I can't understand why he allowed himself to be captured," Stephen whispered while looking carefully into the courtyard to make sure no one else could hear him.

"Neither can I, but I'm sure that Yeshua knows what he is doing." Zach spoke with assurance even though he didn't feel it.

For a while they tried to understand what the various shouts and noises from inside the High Priest's house could mean.

"Zach, look over there. I don't believe it! It's Peter... the man sitting beside the woman who is stoking the fire."

"I see him," Zach murmured. "Peter is very brave to sit there only a few paces away from the guards... I'm surprised that no one has tried to find out who he is yet. His features and beard are so distinctive."

"You are so right! He's not someone who could disappear in a crowd. But how did he pass by the guards at the gate in the first place?"

"Shh, keep in the shadows," Zach nudged Stephen and quickly pointed to their left. A guard was walking around the courtyard and was only a few paces away from them. They froze. Seconds passed. Then someone at the fire made some remark and the guard looked over at the fire and laughed. By then he had passed the pillars. Zach and Stephen didn't budge but kept completely still, hardly breathing. When the guard was a good fifteen paces away the two white-faced followers of Yeshua took some deep breaths.

"That was scary, Zach," said Stephen.

Zach put his finger to his lips and pointed towards the big door at the top of the steps. Someone had just opened it. After a few seconds Zach looked out carefully and then smiled at Stephen. Whoever opened it was gone and had left the door open. The talking in the inner room was now slightly audible. The seconds ticked by and finally Zach whispered, "Someone seems to be shouting."

"And stamping," added Stephen, "or maybe it is just heavy men moving around... more shouting... look Zach... even the guards are listening," Stephen whispered as he looked across at them, hoping that he and Zach were hidden sufficiently in the shadows not to be noticed.

"We're all right," Zach reassured him. Then he turned again towards the door, his ears straining not to miss a sound.

Suddenly all the shouting stopped and one person's voice took control. "Do you hear that, Zach? Someone with a deep voice is laying down the law."

"It's probably Caiaphas. He scares me," said Zach apprehensively.

The deep measured tones continued, followed by a short delay. And then another voice could be heard.

"I think that is Yeshua speaking now," Zach continued with a certain excitement in his voice.

"And now Caiaphas is speaking again," remarked Stephen. "I would love to know what he is saying... Did you hear that? What a shout!"

The two looked at one another in dismay.

"I hope I'm wrong. I thought I heard angry cursing. We should have gone in there," said Zach.

"Zach, you are mad. We could be dead by now if we'd tried that," said Stephen. "The people in there are extremely angry."

Zach cooled down. "You're right, of course, Stephen. But I feel so helpless just sitting here."

"What will James and John do?" Stephen asked, looking at Zach. "That is, if they are in there at all."

"They're not out here so I presume they must be inside. They have great gifts of persuasion." Zach, however, spoke uncertainly.

Outside, at the fire, Peter was being confronted.

"You were with Yeshua of Nazareth," said one of the servant girls of the High Priest, looking at Peter.

"Did you hear that Zach?" asked Stephen.

"I did... What will Peter do now?" replied Zach with great concern.

The girl rolled up her sleeves and stared brazenly at Peter, hands on hips. Peter looked back at her and denied it outright.

"I don't know what you are talking about," Peter said.

Then taking the lead from the first servant girl, another girl began pointing at Peter and, in an equally loud, coarse voice for all to hear, shouted, "He *is* one of them!"

"Who is 'them'?" whispered Stephen. "I thought the authorities were after Yeshua and not his followers as well."

Peter again gruffly denied that he was 'one of them'.

"Peter doesn't stand a chance, everyone is looking at him now," murmured Zach.

A group now confronted Peter. "You can't deny that you are one of them, because you, too, are from Galilee," they accused.

"So what!" said Stephen, "There are hundreds and hundreds of Galileans at the feast? Why pick on Galileans?"

"Peter is cornered, Stephen," Zach muttered, shaking his head. "He is calling down curses on himself, denying any involvement with Yeshua. This is not like Peter, Stephen," Zach spoke slowly, "but I would probably have reacted the same way if I were in his position. We can talk big but when we are confronted directly we give in."

Peter had denied his connections three times before the group were satisfied. Then a trumpet sounded.

"I don't believe it, Zach, it's 'cock crow'... And there is the second trumpet blast."

"How did Yeshua know, Stephen?" Zach's eyes were wide open in wonder. "Remember what Yeshua said, 'I tell you that before the cock crows twice tonight, you will say three times that you do not know me.' He had foreseen all this!"

Just then the sound of soldiers marching came from inside the High Priest's house, growing louder and louder.

"They're coming, Zach," warned Stephen.

Yeshua and two armed guards who looked like gladiators suddenly appeared at the door. Yeshua was in chains and there were spittle marks on his clothes. His face had obviously been punched since it was covered with bruises and blood was trickling down from cuts on his forehead, his right eye and his bottom lip.

"Stephen!" Zach jumped up but Stephen pulled him back.

"Look what they have done." Zach's voice was full of anger. His expression suggested that he wanted to tear someone to pieces. Then his head dropped and his eyes overflowed with heartbroken tears.

The guards and Yeshua stopped still at the top of the steps for a few moments. The metal helmets of the guards reflected the light from the fire and the lanterns in the courtyard. Zach saw that they had swords at their sides and daggers in their belts, and he had to admit that he and Stephen couldn't have achieved anything.

As the guards and Yeshua were walking slowly down the steps Yeshua suddenly stopped just before reaching the floor of the courtyard and looked over to where Peter was standing.

"Stephen, Yeshua is looking directly at Peter," Zach exclaimed. "How did he know Peter was there?"

"Peter is looking at Yeshua too," said Stephen. "Poor Peter. Look at his tears... He remembers what Yeshua had said."

Stephen and Zach looked back at Yeshua, whose expression was one of compassion and forgiveness. The soldiers continued shoving their prisoner, marching him down the last steps, through the courtyard and then out the gate. A large crowd followed, talking, arguing and gesticulating. One or two were silent and seemed very unhappy with the situation.

When the crowd had passed, James and John appeared at the door. They had been with the Sanhedrin in Caiaphas' house. Both of them were looking very angry and, at the same time, helpless. James was obviously working out some plan with John. When Zach and Stephen saw them there, they were delighted and slipped over to them.

"How did you two get here?" said John with concern.

"Mum and Stephen's mum allowed us to come and see what was happening," Zach volunteered.

"Did they realise how dangerous and volatile the whole situation would be?" James asked.

"We hid ourselves beside the pillars," said Zach, keeping up with his brothers as they walked after the crowd. "What happened inside? We heard all the noise and the shouting."

John looked at James and then they decided to tell Zach and Stephen what had happened.

John began. "We managed to get into the meeting room of Caiaphas, thanks to Joseph of Arimathea's connections. All the chief priests and elders and teachers of the Law were there, knowing that Yeshua was to be brought there. We kept a very low profile. It transpired that Judas had given Caiaphas the probable timing of Yeshua's arrival in the olive garden in Gethsemane. So Caiaphas and his friends worked out when Yeshua and the rest of us would likely be asleep."

"They didn't want a riot so the arrest had to be carried out with the utmost secrecy," added James.

"If they struck when everyone was asleep, including Yeshua and ourselves, it would be over and done before anyone knew what had happened." John continued, "The plan more or less worked. When we arrived at Caiaphas' house everything was already in place. Almost all the members of the Sanhedrin were present."

"It began when Caiaphas nodded and evidence for the 'wrongdoings' of Yeshua was introduced. One witness recounted that 'Yeshua of Nazareth' had said, 'I will tear down this Temple which men have made, and after three days I will build one that is not made by men.' When that made no sense to anyone, more 'witnesses' were introduced. They made other accusations, which were obviously concocted. Some people at the meeting took them seriously but others just laughed at their absurdity. There were many very smart lawyers there and under scrutiny none of it held up. Some of the elders were annoyed, believing that the whole thing was a political set-up and had nothing to do with either the Temple or our way of life.

However, realising that he might be losing his 'prey', Caiaphas, in a cynical and superior voice, asked Yeshua, 'Are you the Messiah, the Son of the Blessed God?'

Up to that point Yeshua had said nothing at all, but to everyone's surprise, he calmly answered, 'I am.'"

"Did Yeshua really say that?" asked Zach in astonishment.

"Yes, he did. It certainly removed all doubt as to who he is... and then he quoted the prophet Daniel, 'You will all see the Son of Man seated at the right side of the Almighty and coming with the clouds of heaven.'

"Well, on hearing that, the High Priest felt he had won, but, to make sure, he ripped his High Priest's robes, which indicated that Yeshua was guilty of blasphemy.

"'We don't need any more witnesses!' Caiaphas said. 'You heard his blasphemy. What is your verdict?'

"It was a clever act and most of the assembly fell for it. They let out a shout saying that Yeshua deserved to die. No doubt there were people planted there who were primed to call for his death. Nevertheless, what happened was appalling. Believe it or not, a number of these exalted people began spitting at Yeshua and, having blindfolded him, they hit him with their fists and shouted, 'Guess who hit you?'

"It became a free-for-all, with the attendants also landing blows on Yeshua. But Yeshua said nothing more." John looked around to see how far they had come, not wanting to lose sight of Yeshua and the guards.

"It's amazing what people will do when they are in a mob," said James. "I really couldn't believe what I saw. In fact, I still can't believe what is happening now."

"When Yeshua said that he was the Messiah, should they not have been delighted that the Messiah had come at last?" asked Zach.

"Zach," said John, "he is not the kind of Messiah they were expecting. Yeshua isn't interested in power and might, but in service and helping others, all peoples, including non-Jews, especially those who have very little... Look, they've stopped!"

CHAPTER 34

"Marcellus, what is wrong?" Pontius Pilate was fuming as he began putting on his toga. "Do you know what time of night it is? It's bad enough to have to come here to Jerusalem for this feast but to be woken in the middle of the night by these troublesome, fanatic people is just not good enough. Can't Caiaphas deal with whatever is troubling him?"

"It seems not, Pilate," said Marcellus, looking directly at Pilate. "This case seems quite different. I think that Caiaphas is particularly worried about a prophet called Yeshua."

"A prophet? Another of them! Surely that is a religious matter and not a political matter. These people are intolerable." Pilate was furious as he spoke, but continued putting on his military attire.

"You are new to this place, Marcellus," Pilate continued, "so let me fill you in on some of the problems I have had with these Jewish people. When I was appointed Prefect of Judea, I knew that they would not allow Roman soldiers to carry Roman standards, even though we Romans could always do so elsewhere. So, as a compromise, I decided to arrive in the dark of night. Someone, however, must have seen us and a riot broke out... Also, 'graven images' like the many statues we have in Rome are not allowed here either, so I refrained from putting up statues or images in public. Inside this palace, however, I put up the name of Augustus in golden letters, but it was inside my palace and carefully out of sight of the people. But, as always happens, someone found out about it and reported me to Rome. Needless to say, I was furious that the Emperor had been contacted, putting me in a bad light – but they knew that. Am I boring you?"

"No, Pilate, this is fascinating and it's good that I should know," Marcellus responded, listening carefully to Pilate.

"Another incident occurred," continued Pilate, "because I wanted to increase the water supply to the city. The city was expanding and more water was badly needed so I put my heart into the project. I got excellent Roman engineers to help build it and, as you know, our engineers are the best there are. However, the project went over budget and the leaders of the city refused to pay. So, instead of rejoicing at having a wonderful water supply there was another riot. Now, Marcellus, how does one deal with riots? My first thought was to wipe out large numbers of them with good, Roman thoroughness. However, I decided to be less aggressive and more reasonable. I also feared more reports to Rome and the Emperor. So, instead, I sent soldiers without uniform, in plain-clothes who, without bloodshed, succeeded in quelling the riot. I was delighted with my men but – and you won't believe this – when the rioters realized what had happened they were furious and were reported to me as saying, 'He wouldn't even let us be martyred.'"

Marcellus laughed. "What a people!"

"Marcellus," continued Pilate, "if Caiaphas is coming here tonight he probably wants me to have his prophet eliminated... I hate this job, Marcellus... can you understand that?"

"I certainly can. From what you tell me, your job is a poisoned chalice." Marcellus began to walk towards the balcony.

"How much longer before they arrive, Marcellus?" Pilate yawned.

"I think they should be here soon, it is after 'cock crow'... actually they're here now. They're approaching the main gates already. They have a prisoner in chains. I suppose it is the prophet who is causing them trouble."

When the entourage arrived, Yeshua was put standing before Pilate, who had reluctantly come out to meet the High Priest and his chained prophet. Marcellus stood there with Pilate, flanked by a number of soldiers in full battle outfit, with spears, swords and daggers.

"I have never seen Pilate before," said Zach.

"There isn't an ounce of fat anywhere on his body, just muscle. But he doesn't seem to be a happy person this morning. I suppose he is annoyed at being woken up to more Jerusalem trouble," Stephen looked with simmering anger at Pilate and the soldiers.

"He looks ruthless," remarked Zach, "and if Rome wasn't looking over his shoulder he could easily order his soldiers in Jerusalem to scatter the crowd here, not caring how many people die or are injured. He's probably saying to himself, 'These people deserve whatever happens to them.'"

"I couldn't agree more," said Stephen, still looking at Pilate with disgust.

"Well, Caiaphas, what is the problem... at this hour of the night?" asked Pilate.

Caiaphas smiled, walked over to Pilate and spoke quietly to him. As they spoke, Pilate looked at Yeshua now and then. Caiaphas was evidently explaining to him why Yeshua was so dangerous.

"But, Caiaphas," Pilate spoke a little louder so that he could be heard, "surely we are talking here about internal Jewish matters? This isn't political."

Caiaphas spoke to him again in a low voice so nobody could hear.

"The Nazarene looks to me like a harmless poor man. And you have messed him up I see," said Pilate, again loud enough to be heard.

Pilate looked more carefully at Yeshua with his blood-stained garment, his face covered with bruises, gashes and large blotches of blood where the blows from the fists of priests and elders and the sticks of the guards had landed.

"I suppose Pilate is used to soldiers and their floggings, not to mention battle wounds and scars," said Zach.

Pilate turned to Marcellus and suggested barely audibly, "Let's annoy these people." Then he spoke to Yeshua, "Are you the 'King of the Jews'?"

There was no laughter, however. Pilate had misjudged the situation. Yeshua looked up with gentleness and said to Pilate, "So you say."

Realising that Yeshua had not answered the question, the chief priests began making all sorts of accusations against him. They were all nonsense and Yeshua remained silent during all their ranting. So Pilate addressed Yeshua again, "Aren't you going to answer them? Listen to all their accusations!"

But to the astonishment of even Pilate, Yeshua remained silent. Zach dejectedly said to Stephen, "This reminds me of Isaiah the Prophet's words, 'We despised him and rejected him.'"

"You are so right," Stephen quietly replied.

Meanwhile Pilate had a brief private discussion with Marcellus who had been sent by Rome to help Pilate in his difficult mission. Marcellus was known to be a highly intelligent and resourceful person. Pilate, listening to his suggestions, began to acknowledge to himself that his second-in-command was clever.

"You are right, Marcellus," he murmured.

"Caiaphas," said Pilate, turning back and addressing the chief priests, "since Yeshua is from Galilee, he comes under Herod Antipas' jurisdiction and not under mine, so I think that it is right that you bring the prophet to him."

Caiaphas couldn't believe what he was hearing and was furious. He was losing time. In a few hours Jerusalem would begin to wake up and the followers of Yeshua might find out what was happening. Hiding his disgust, he turned and left Pilate.

"We have to go to Herod's palace. Go quickly!" Caiaphas said to his guards and the others who were there.

The members of the Sanhedrin and the others who had joined the mob were furious at this turn of events. What now? They moved away and began walking to the Hasmonean Palace where Herod Antipas stayed while he was in Jerusalem.

"We seem to be going to Herod's lair now... from one ruthless man to another," Stephen said with both anger and fear. "Will we ever wake up from this nightmare, Zach?"

Zach was lost in thought and didn't immediately answer. Then he felt a tap on his shoulder.

"Ruth, you're here!" Fear and terror made their hugs extra emotional. Then Zach saw his mother, along with Ruth's and Stephen's, a little distance away.

"You have all come I see. What is happening is absolutely terrible," Zach explained. He noticed that Ruth was a little pale and he wondered if she were all right.

"Are you sure you want to be here, Ruth?" Zach asked as he looked into her eyes and moved a stray hair from her face.

Ruth smiled. "I must be here. I owe Yeshua my life," she said. Zach knew then that if he thought *he* was a follower of Yeshua, Ruth was even more so.

Soon the crowd had moved into a large open square in front of Herod's palace, a mighty building built in earlier times by the Hasmonean or Maccabean kings.

"This palace is certainly a sign of wealth, power and might," said Stephen. There were lights all around it and Herod's soldiers were keeping watch.

"Look, Zach... the Temple," Ruth had just realised how near it was to Herod's palace.

"Isn't it strange that our priests and elders," asked Zach with sadness, "many of whom are great people, are trying to convict Yeshua of crimes he did not commit, all in view of the Temple?"

Ruth stood beside him in silence. 'He is right,' she thought.

"We'll hardly see Herod at this hour of the night," remarked Stephen cynically.

"I am sure he has been warned of Yeshua's arrival, Stephen," replied Zach, and sure enough, Herod soon appeared and Yeshua had to face him. However, Herod was unimpressed with the 'crimes' that were listed against him.

"I really believe that Herod knows that Yeshua is innocent and will have nothing to do with punishing someone who he probably has written off as 'this rather messed-up man from Galilee'," said Zach bitterly, his suppressed anger evident.

"What is Herod doing now? Look! He has decided to put a kind of purple kingly robe on Yeshua to mock him... Look at Herod, he is laughing!" cried Stephen. He was furious. "If only I had a brick I might remove that smirk from his face."

"You wouldn't, Stephen," Ruth reproved.

"I said 'might', Ruth," explained Stephen with a wry smile. "I certainly feel as if I would."

Herod showed mocking disdain for the mob and with a sudden movement he turned his back on everyone and disappeared back into his palace. Some people jeered at him but it didn't last long. Everyone knew that this could have deathly consequences.

"How is it that our nation has such shallow people as Governors?" asked Zach, as he saw Herod disappearing.

The three friends had no alternative but to accompany the mob on their way back to Pilate's Palace. Pilate, on seeing Yeshua wearing a kingly robe was mildly amused at first, but then realised that this meant that he, Pilate, would have to make the final decision regarding this prophet from Galilee.

"Pilate is not too happy that it is he who has to deal with Yeshua," Zach said.

"I wonder what he is going to do now," said Ruth as she tightly held on to Zach's arm.

"Look Zach! There's another man in chains. He is a few paces to the other side of Pilate. Who is he? He looks really rough. I certainly wouldn't like to have an argument with him!" Stephen said, worried by this new turn of events.

"That man is called Barabbas," explained an elderly woman with a hoarse, deep voice. She was standing behind Stephen, rubbing tears from her eyes. "He is a murderer. He killed someone in the recent riots; whereas Yeshua, Yeshua is a good man, a kind man, a loving man... he cured my son last year."

Ruth, seeing her distress, put her arms around her. The woman, her head on Ruth's shoulder, began to sob. "How can they be doing this?" she said.

Pilate, meanwhile, stood there, with Yeshua on one side and Barabbas on the other, along with the armed guards. After a few minutes, Marcellus raised his hand. It was a signal for everyone to be silent. Immediately the crowd became quiet and Pilate spoke.

"Do you want me to set the 'King of the Jews' free for you?"

A good number of the crowd cheered in agreement, and it seemed that the whole High Priestly plan to have him punished by Rome was in tatters.

"Zach, Ruth, Yeshua is not a king as they understand a king and he is not a threat to anyone. He will be set free!" Stephen was delighted.

Just then a large group in the crowd started calling for the release of Barabbas. Zach turned and looked at his two companions. He didn't need to say anything. He was beside himself with rage.

"Zach, you can't do anything now," Ruth said, holding him firmly by the arm.

"How could they? Even Pilate believes it is all nonsense," cried Zach, breathless with fury.

"What, then, do you want me to do with the one you call the 'King of the Jews'?" Pilate continued in a loud voice.

The gang looked in dismay around the crowd for a reaction.

"Surely they must realize that Pilate is saying to them 'Wake up, you stupid people, this miserable man here who is dressed in kingly robes is a 'nobody', let him go!'" Zach stared at Pilate and the soldiers and the people. And then a cry came from one person and then from another and then from several, "Crucify him!"

Pilate was shocked, as was Marcellus beside him. Ruth felt faint and almost fell, but Zach caught her and held her tightly. Stephen gasped.

"This can't be happening!" Zach felt sick, his heart was pounding in his ears.

"But what crime has he committed?" Pilate shouted. "I cannot find anything he has done to deserve death! I will have him whipped and set him free."

The shouting of the crowd got louder. Pilate looked at them with disbelief and disgust.

"What is Yeshua being whipped for if Pilate can find no crime he has committed? ... I'm sure that this crowd is being paid to shout out, and no doubt Caiaphas and his henchmen are behind it," Zach said, with fury and frustration in his voice and tears in his eyes.

"Pilate is releasing Barabbas," Stephen said through his half-clenched teeth. "Look at the smirk on Barabbas' face."

Stephen watched to see where Barabbas was gone but he just seemed to disappear. At the same time, Yeshua had been taken away by some soldiers. Pilate was having his order of 'whipping' carried out.

'What is happening?' Claudia, Pilate's wife, asked herself. She called for her maid, Rosa. "What is happening, Rosa?" asked Claudia, "I heard terrible noises downstairs."

"Madam, they brought in a prisoner and were whipping him."

"I hope it wasn't the prophet from Galilee, Yeshua of Nazareth," she said.

"Yes, I think it was the prophet. And they treated him very badly indeed."

"That is terrible, Rosa, I believe he is a good man, a man of God," Claudia said. "What did they do to him? Tell me, Rosa, and don't hide anything. Remember I am the wife of a soldier and have already seen dreadful things. There is also another reason I ask you. I had a terrible dream about that prophet. But, first, tell me what happened to him."

"Well, I was almost asleep in my room, but I heard such a racket that I got up to see what was happening. It was terrible, really, really terrible. The soldiers took the prophet into an inner part of the palace and stripped him and then scourged him viciously. Any ordinary person would surely have died as a result of the lashes. It was evil, pure evil. I don't know much about rules and regulations but I believe that for Roman citizens the scourging is normally confined to thirty-nine lashes. But in the prophet's case, since he is not a Roman, they just lashed and lashed him until he collapsed, almost dead. He hung there swinging on the ropes with which they had tied him naked to a pole. The gashes all over his back and sides and shoulders and neck were oozing blood. And throughout all this the prophet said nothing. He didn't complain and didn't get angry. To me he looked like a poor sheep that was being slaughtered."

"You said he didn't get angry – yes, he is a man of God," said Claudia, "but continue, Rosa."

"Seeing him only half-conscious, the soldiers poured water on him to try and revive him. They were hoping he wasn't dead, but from what I had seen, it wouldn't have worried them too much. However, the prophet did slowly come round, though he was still bleeding a great deal. After some unrepeatable jokes as to whether they would continue or not, the soldier in charge decided to dress the prophet up in a scarlet robe. Some others twisted some thorns into a crown and put it on his head. They roared raucously then and began mocking him. They saluted him and bowed down to him. I heard one of them saying, 'Long live the 'King of the

Jews'!' Then they spat on him and even struck his thorn-crowned head. The pain must have been indescribable." At that stage Rosa broke down and cried bitterly.

"Rosa, thank you so much for telling me. I have one more thing to ask of you. I want you to bring a letter to my husband. Wait here and I will write it." Claudia went to her room and wrote, 'Pilate, have nothing to do with that innocent man, because in a dream last night, I suffered much on account of him.'

When she had finished her letter she brought it back to her maid and said, "Now go, Rosa, and quickly give it to my husband. Go!" Rosa wiped away her tears and ran as fast as she could.

When they had had their cruel fun, the soldiers brought Yeshua back once more to Pilate. When Ruth saw him she screamed, but the sound was lost in the baying of the crowd.

Zach felt sure that Ruth should not be there. But there was no way out.

As Yeshua stood there, Pilate, stony-faced, stared at the crowd with ill-concealed disdain.

"Maybe the sight of Yeshua will change the mind of the crowd. I think that is what Pilate is hoping will happen," said Stephen hopefully.

Just then Rosa appeared and handed one of the soldiers the letter for Pilate. Pilate read it and looked questioningly at Yeshua.

"I hope the scourging has done its job and they will have pity on this Nazarene," Pilate whispered to Marcellus over his shoulder.

Just then a voice howled out, "If you set him free, that means that you are not the Emperor's friend! Anyone who claims to be a king is a rebel against the Emperor!"

"That's it," said Zach slowly. "It's over. Yeshua will be crucified. Pilate won't want a complaint sent to Rome."

Pilate became furious. "Here is your king!" he cried, hoping that the mob would see how stupid the whole case was and just go away.

The crowd roared back, "Kill him! Kill him! Crucify him!"

"Do you want me to crucify your king?" Pilate asked, his mouth a cynical wince, his hatred for the mob becoming more and more obvious.

But the crowd wouldn't let up. "We have no king but the Emperor!"

Pilate turned pale and stared at the crowd. He was just about keeping his temper in control.

'Maybe Caiaphas has his reasons,' he said to himself, 'but what about Claudia's dream?' He turned to Marcellus and asked, "What do you think? Can we get out of this?"

Marcellus peered at the crowd with searching, determined eyes. Like Pilate, he knew they were in deep trouble. The Roman governance of Israel was under threat. "As far as I can see we have only two choices," he said. "Disperse this uncouth mob, which they deserve, and risk a riot, or – grant them their wishes. The prophet is probably not guilty. But it's Caiaphas' call, so we can blame him and his colleagues."

Pilate acknowledged the clear reasoning of Marcellus. He was right.

He then slowly sat down to make his solemn judgment. When they saw him seated, the crowd became tensely silent. Had they gone too far? Will Pilate call in the soldiers, who could ruthlessly scatter them with many casualties and maybe even some deaths? They waited. A few isolated shouts were quickly silenced. Pilate, prolonging the silence, signaled to one of his guards to bring over a basin of water. The soldier brought water and a towel. Without looking at the mob, Pilate slowly washed his hands and dried them. Then, as the soldier walked away with the bowl and towel, Pilate turned to the people and picking out a group of high priests who were there, he said clearly and without inflection, "I am not responsible for the death of this man. This is your doing."

There was a stunned silence. What would happen now? Then, like the screech of a predator bird, someone screamed, "Let the responsibility for his death fall on us and on our children!"

Pilate with evident disdain looked over to where the shout came from and confirmed to Marcellus, "They have understood our message."

Meanwhile Ruth, with horror, said, "Did you hear that?"

"I did," replied Zach, "but look at Pilate. He is blaming our people, not himself... I suppose in some ways he is right."

Pilate nodded and the soldiers took Yeshua away. The crowd became silent. The result of their shouting for Yeshua's death became real.

"Look at them dragging Yeshua down the stairs. What a ruthless, vicious and savage group!" said Stephen, hoarse with anger.

Zach, clearly distressed, resolutely stated, "We need to stay with Yeshua until the very end."

"Zach, is there any way that they could change their minds?" asked Ruth, her dark eyes fixed on the door underneath the balcony where Pilate and Yeshua had been standing.

"Pilate is the highest authority in our land and therefore there is no appeal. And I don't think there is any delay system," replied Zach, as he too watched the door, waiting for Yeshua. They waited and waited, and Ruth looked at Zach again silently with the same question in her eyes. Zach shook his head signalling that it was now just a matter of time.

CHAPTER 35

Two soldiers appeared first, one carrying a sign.

"Look at that sign!" Stephen addressed his words to no one in particular. "'Yeshua of Nazareth, King of the Jews' and in three languages so that nobody will miss the point." Then he turned to Zach and Ruth. "Pilate is certainly having the last say. He is jeering our leaders. What do you think?" he asked.

"You are absolutely right," said Zach, "the sign is normally supposed to inform people of what the person did wrong but this one only says that Yeshua is from Nazareth and is 'King of the Jews'. It is all a horrible political game."

"Oh look! Yeshua is coming out the door... He is carrying a huge crossbeam. They *are* going to crucify him!" Zach held Ruth protectively as he spoke. Holding her helped him control his anger. As a result he was able to watch and then follow Yeshua as he walked, without shouting and screaming at the Romans.

The gang followed Yeshua, the soldiers and the mob, in silence - broken occasionally by small sobs from Ruth. It was difficult for the three friends to see Yeshua all the time, but since the two boys were taller than average, they were able to keep Ruth informed of what was happening.

"I can see why they sent five soldiers," Stephen said, as he stood on his toes to see better. "There could be a mini-riot on their hands and it would take at least five soldiers to deal with it... The centurion is obviously a professional... Authority oozes out of him."

Although the centurion was of average size he looked like someone who knew what iron discipline was all about. He was used to giving orders that would be obeyed immediately.

"I can see Yeshua," said Ruth. "Oh no! he has just fallen. Zach, he looks absolutely terrible. I hardly recognize him. He is covered in blood. There are red and blue marks all over his face and his hair is covered in clotted blood – he has hardly any strength left. He will surely die before he gets to wherever they are taking him."

Yeshua was being flogged and ordered to get up, even though he had hardly the strength to put one foot in front of the other. Zach noticed that one of the teachers of the Law was quietly smiling. He wanted to pick up a stone and fire it at him but he realised that Ruth might also suffer if the soldiers intervened.

By now they had guessed that the crucifixion group was heading for the Gennath Gate. "The soldiers are going this way to get out of the city and to avoid the huge numbers here for the festival," Zach said.

"Zach, I could never have dreamt that the soldiers could be so evil," said Ruth, as she was nearly knocked down by a man trying to get a better view.

Zach commented, "The soldiers are a ruthless and cruel lot but I suppose they are just doing their job. For them Yeshua is a convicted criminal."

Zach, however, wanted to get closer to Yeshua. He looked around and suddenly whispered to his two companions, "Quick, follow me. There is a side street here. If we take it we can get nearer to Yeshua."

They pushed their way through the crowd with Zach on one side and Stephen on the other and Ruth just behind them, shielded from the pressure.

"That's better," whispered Zach. "Yeshua will appear in a few seconds and there are only those four people in front of us... there he is... he looks absolutely dreadful!"

Yeshua staggered. He was struggling with the crossbeam. It was too heavy for him to carry. Zach wanted to run and help him but Ruth and Stephen held him back.

"You can't, Zach," they both said simultaneously.

Then Yeshua fell. He wasn't able to break the fall, so he fell on his face and the beam fell on his back and shoulder and banged the side of his head. He lay completely still.

"No!" Zach swallowed a shout. "This is barbaric!" Tears filled his eyes, his breathing became faster and he began muttering under his breath.

Ruth, holding on to him, whispered, "Yeshua might be dead... it would be better for him if he were."

But the soldiers just cursed the fallen Yeshua and pulled and dragged at him and he moved a little. Then, somehow, he struggled to his feet again and after getting back his balance, he staggered on.

"Look over there," Ruth pointed, "it's Yeshua's mother... Yeshua has turned towards her. He seems to recognize her. Look, he has greeted her..."

"But look at his face now," Stephen murmured. "He is clearly in a sea of pain."

"And look at the soldiers," Zach remarked. "I believe they know that Yeshua may not make it to the place of crucifixion. They seem to be looking for someone to help Yeshua with the crossbeam."

"I'll go," said Zach, and he began pushing his way forward. But by the time he had gone a few steps the soldiers had caught hold of a passer-by, and had forced him to take up one end of the heavy beam.

Zach seeing that the job he wanted was gone, slowly stepped back again beside Stephen and Ruth. "Zach," comforted Ruth, "you did your best. At least Yeshua has some help now."

The man helping Yeshua was of dark complexion and fairly bald. He had a round face that suggested that in normal times he would be a happy person. Not now, however, as he was landed with a very difficult task.

As they arrived at the Gennath Gate, there was suddenly confusion.

"There seems to be something wrong," said Stephen. "We've stopped."

"I think that the early morning crowds are coming in the gate," suggested Zach, "and we are going out... The soldiers will sort it out."

"Look!" said Ruth. "There's a group of women near the gate who are crying. I don't recognise them. I wonder who they are."

"Ruth, Stephen, come this way," said Zach. "We'll try again to get nearer to Yeshua."

The three of them ran up a small pathway between houses and were shortly right beside the Gennath Gate and could see Yeshua.

"He is stopping. I think he is about to say something to those women," said Stephen.

"Where does he get the strength?" said Ruth as she gently pushed a little nearer to listen.

"Women of Jerusalem! Don't cry for me... but for yourselves... and your children. For if... such things... are done ... when the wood is green... what will happen... when it is dry?"

"What did he say, Ruth?" Both Zach and Stephen asked her. Ruth was nearer to Yeshua than they were.

"He told the women," Ruth said, wiping away tears, "not to cry for him but for themselves and for their children." She shook her head, and continued, "He also said something about when the wood is green and when it is dry. I didn't pick that up too well."

In the end, everyone was surprised at how quickly the soldiers and Yeshua got through the gate. The soldiers were certainly making things happen. Nobody would dare stand in their way. Now, on the right of Yeshua was the city wall, and towering behind the wall was the Temple. To the north of the Temple stood the Antonia Fortress where the Roman soldiers were normally based.

The procession, which it now had become, moved slowly but soon it turned left and into a quarry area with a small hill called Golgotha.

"They are going up that hill," said Stephen. "How will Yeshua be able to climb it?"

"No! No! No!" said Zach, putting his hand up to his face when he saw that Yeshua had fallen again.

"This time it is worse," said Stephen. Ruth and Zach turned away from looking at the scene.

"Endless curses should be showered down on those who are responsible for this," added Zach.

Zach and Ruth turned back to look, only to see more brutal beating, pulling and lifting of Yeshua by the soldiers.

"How can Yeshua get up again? He should be dead," said Stephen. "Look! The soldiers are grudgingly giving him some help."

"For what, Stephen?" Zach asked in dismay, nodding towards some poles already stuck in the ground at the top of the hill. "For that?"

"Zach, your mother and my mother are over there. I think they are asking me to join them," said Ruth.

Zach looked over and saw the women gesturing for Ruth to come over to them. "Go! Ruth," said Zach. "Our mothers want to have you with them." She squeezed his hand and ran quickly over to her mother.

Meanwhile, Stephen had been so engrossed in watching what was happening that when he turned back to Zach, he saw that Ruth was gone.

"Zach, where is Ruth?" Stephen's face was filled with fright.

"She's gone over to her mother and the other women who are over there." Zach pointed as he spoke.

"Ah yes, I see them. And John, your brother, is with them," said Stephen.

"What?" said Zach, hoping it was true ... "Yes, he's there. I knew he would make it in the end. I wonder where James is."

"Look, Yeshua has managed to climb the hill! It's incredible. And now the soldiers are offering him a drink," said Stephen.

"It's probably to ease the pain. It seems that that is normal," murmured Zach. Although they were at the bottom of the small hill both Zach and Stephen were standing only about twenty yards away from Yeshua.

"Yeshua has refused the drink," Stephen said shaking his head in wonder.

"Look at them now! How utterly crass they are! They are stripping Yeshua of his clothes. They are trying to remove his dignity ... but they won't succeed," Zach cried.

As though they were ripping paper off a parcel, they stripped Yeshua of his garments. Then, as Yeshua lay on the ground naked, one of the soldiers bent down and with nails and a hammer began nailing his hands, near the wrists, to the crossbeam. Zach and Stephen watched it all, white with horror and sick with anger. And then Zach felt a hand on his shoulder. It was Ruth, and with her were the other women. Zach began to cry bitterly and Ruth caught hold of him and brought his head towards her shoulder. Stephen, at the same time turned to his mother, and he too put his head on her shoulder, like he had as a child, and cried inconsolably.

The soldiers then tied Yeshua's arms to the crossbeam so that he couldn't break loose.

"What a needless precaution," murmured Zach, as he lifted his head to watch despite his tears. "Yeshua has hardly enough energy to breathe, let alone break loose."

Then, with a ladder and ropes, the soldiers pulled Yeshua up the centre pole, along with the crossbeam to which he was nailed and tied. They firmly tied the crossbeam to the pole, and then nailed Yeshua's feet to the upright pole. They used only one long nail that went right through both his feet just below his ankles.

"This is just evil, pure evil ... and look ... the political game still continues. They are putting up Pilate's sign to get back at the High Priest," Zach took a deep breath and hung his head.

Just then Zach, Ruth, Stephen and all the women looked upwards in complete astonishment. Yeshua was speaking quietly.

"Forgive them, Father! They don't know what they are doing."

Zach was speechless. He looked at Yeshua, covered in bruises, blood oozing slowly from his hands and feet, from the marks of the lashes he had received, and from his head, caused by the crown of multiple thorns. His face too was battered and bruised, and his torso naked.

Zach, his voice hoarse, said "How can Yeshua forgive them? How can he?" Then he turned and said to Ruth, "For me it would be impossible. I would be working out ways to get revenge."

"But you remember, Zach, Yeshua told us to forgive seventy-times seven times," Ruth reminded him.

As all this was happening Yeshua's own people were singing happily in the Temple, while their brother, the 'beloved son' of God, the Messiah, was being crucified.

"What a travesty," sighed Stephen, shaking his head wearily.

"Zach, Stephen, look! Some of the passers-by are laughing at Yeshua," Ruth looked at the people, horrified. Sure enough they were laughing at Yeshua and mocking him, as they passed by along the road towards the Gennath Gate.

"I don't believe it," said Zach, his voice loud and angry, but then Stephen and Ruth realized that he was referring to something else that he had noticed.

"Look! Soldiers are bringing out... I think it is two men... I wonder if they are going to crucify them alongside Yeshua."

"They are turning this way," said Stephen.

Everyone watched as two men were brought past them, up the hill and then were ignominiously crucified beside Yeshua. When the soldiers were finished, there were three crosses, with Yeshua in the middle.

Zach said, "The authorities have surely arranged this in order to lessen the importance of Yeshua's death, and to make him seem just like any other condemned person."

Stephen, realizing that Zach was right, was beside himself with anger. Then he heard jeering coming from behind him. It was the chief priests and teachers of the Law. Stephen bent down hurriedly and picked up a stone and was about to throw it at them but John caught him by the wrist.

"It's not worth it, Stephen. It will only make things worse," John said quietly.

"But John, they are jeering and laughing and making jokes about Yeshua. Can you not hear them?" Stephen argued.

"Of course, we all can. But like Yeshua just said, they don't know what they are doing. Let's ignore them and just be here for Yeshua until the end."

Time passed and they remained with Yeshua. He was finding it harder and harder to breathe. He had to lift himself up on his pierced feet to get some air and then he would drop back down again. The pain of it all was obviously beyond any words. And then something totally unexpected happened.

"Aren't you the Messiah? Save yourself and us," taunted one of the men being crucified with Yeshua.

Before Yeshua could reply the other man being crucified answered him, "Don't you fear God? We received the same sentence as he did, but we are getting what we deserve. He, however, has done no wrong."

After that immense effort of speaking, the man struggled for breath and in a weaker voice addressed Yeshua, "Remember me, Yeshua, when you come as King."

"I think he knows Yeshua," whispered Ruth.

"I think you are right," answered Zach. "I wonder how."

As they watched they noticed that Yeshua was trying to get enough breath to answer. It was such a struggle for him. He had to lift himself up again on the nail that pierced his feet. Finally, he answered the criminal who had asked to be remembered.

"I promise you... that today... you will be with me... in Paradise."

Having said that, Yeshua's body fell down again on his pierced feet, and pain seared through his body. It was written all over his face.

"Zach," Ruth spoke with quiet conviction as she watched. "Yeshua has come to call sinners. And now he is dying for us sinners. It is all so clear now."

"I agree with you, totally," Zach affirmed in the same tone, "but it is an abomination that it should need this barbaric death to teach us that. I wonder if there could have been another way."

Stephen turned to them both and added his thoughts. "You know, I have just been thinking that Isaiah half-explains what is happening here. Somewhere in his writings, he quoted God as saying, 'My thoughts are not like yours, and my ways are different from yours. As high as the heavens are above the earth, so high are my ways above your ways, my thoughts above your thoughts.' We are so small, so limited, so lacking in understanding. Yeshua is right. We are like small children… clueless." Stephen shook his head as he spoke. He was beginning to find some meaning in it all.

Ruth quietly added, "I actually hope that Yeshua will die soon. His suffering is unbearable."

Three hours passed. Then, at the sixth hour, a great darkness came over the city. It was most unusual. It seemed to be a kind of sandstorm coming in from the desert nearby. The dust made the whole place eerily dark. The people gathered there became very silent. The air was oppressive.

"He's choking for air," Zach said and then fell back into silence, his thoughts heavy with confusion and desperation.

Ruth suddenly tightened her grip on his arm and nodded towards the foot of the cross.

"The soldiers are gambling for Yeshua's blood-soaked garment," she said, "the seamless one that his mother made for him." She lapsed into silence again.

Because of their discussion, John was already halfway up the hill before they noticed. He was motioning to the centurion that he wanted to talk to him.

"What is John doing?" asked Ruth. "Will the centurion attack him?"

The centurion nodded at John and beckoned him to come over, then listened to what John had to say. The centurion looked down towards the three friends and the women who were near them and nodded his head.

"Has John asked for something?" wondered Stephen.

"I think so. He seems to be looking at Yeshua's mother, but I'm not sure," replied Zach.

John came back down the hill and spoke to the women who were gathered together. After a few moments four of them were climbing the hill with John – Yeshua's mother Mary, Mary of Magdala, Salome and Clophas' wife, Mary.

"The centurion may believe that Yeshua's crucifixion was unjust," Ruth said quietly.

"Look! I think that Yeshua sees his mother," said Zach.

John stood with his arms around Yeshua's mother, who was so distressed that she was hardly able to look at her son in his agony. "Your mother is here, Yeshua," John said to Yeshua.

Yeshua, despite his terrible pain, looked down tenderly and then, with huge effort, raised his body on his pierced feet, in order to get some air, and spoke. "He is your son," he said, looking at his mother and referring to John.

Then, lifting his body once more for air, he looked at John. "She is your mother," he said.

"Yeshua isn't thinking of himself at all. He wants his mother to be safe," murmured Zach. "It seems that my brother John is to look after Mary from now on."

"What a gift for your family!" said Ruth.

"Yes, but at what a price," answered Zach grimly.

"Look! Yeshua has become unconscious, I think," said Stephen. They looked at Yeshua to see if it was a coma or possibly death.

"This must be terrible for his mother," said Zach, "absolutely terrible. I can't begin to imagine it."

Stephen was angry. "Some people are saying that God is punishing Yeshua. That God is behind these events and is on the side of the chief priests and teachers of the Law. Yes, some are saying that God is angry with Yeshua. Do you hear them?"

Zach caught Stephen by the shoulder and strongly remonstrated. "We know that is just nonsense! I might have believed that before, but not now. Yeshua has shown us what God is really like."

Just then, as if Yeshua had heard what was being said, he cried out, "My God, my God, why did you abandon me?"

Zach looked up in complete dismay at Yeshua.

'What can that mean?' he asked himself. 'Am I wrong in believing in him?'

Then a look of understanding came over his face. He had just worked it out. He had no idea how it came to him but he wanted to tell the other two and said, "Yeshua is reciting David's song! It says, 'But I am no longer a human being; I am a worm. Despised and scorned by everyone! All who see me make fun of me; they stick out their tongues and shake their heads,' then, 'You relied on the Lord, why doesn't he save you?'"

"You are right, Zach!" said Stephen really pleased at this insight.

Stephen then continued, "And, the song ends in triumph! 'Future generations will serve him; they will speak of the Lord to the coming generation. People not yet born will be told: The Lord saved his people.'"

"The Lord saved his people," Ruth repeated with confidence.

"Did Yeshua just say that he was thirsty?" asked Stephen. "Yes, look! One of the soldiers has a sponge dipped in wine on a stick and is holding it up to Yeshua's lips."

"He seems to have accepted it," added Zach.

They then waited and waited. The air was very heavy, and dark clouds appeared. "It's very dark," said Ruth, "I feel that a very severe storm is threatening."

Just then Yeshua opened his eyes as if someone was speaking to him. He seemed to be listening carefully. After a few seconds, with an expression of great joy on his blood-stained, bruised and battered face he said, quite loudly,

"It is accomplished!"

"Look at the joy on Yeshua's face!" said Zach, in tears. Looking around, he saw that Ruth, Stephen, and all those with them were equally emotional. Then they heard Yeshua whisper to the One who was obviously there with him, "Father, into your hands I commend my spirit."

At that, Yeshua's head fell on his chest. There was no more struggling for air, no more involuntary spasms. His whole body was still.

"He is gone from us!" Zach sobbed. Holding each other, the gang cried bitterly.

When they looked up again towards the body of Yeshua hanging motionless on the cross, they saw the centurion with unusual gentleness and compassion gently touch Yeshua's mother's shoulder. "Certainly, he was a good man!" he stated.

At that, heavy drops of rain began to fall, and lightening lit up the sky. Zach quietly said, "You were right, Ruth. A huge storm has come."

CHAPTER 36

The guards at Pilate's palace, seeing Joseph of Arimathea and Nicodemus Ben Gurion approach, saluted them and allowed them entry into the palace. Marcellus, Pilate's right-hand man, saw them too.

"Good afternoon gentlemen, can I help you?"

"We are hoping to see the Governor for just a few moments, if he could possibly spare us the time," replied Joseph with due deference.

"Joseph and Nicodemus, welcome!" It was Pilate who spoke from a balcony overlooking the stairwell. The two visitors looked up at the Governor. "Come up!" Pilate commanded.

Joseph and Nicodemus climbed the steps, led by Marcellus.

"What can I do for you, gentlemen? Don't tell me. It's about Yeshua from Nazareth, the 'King of the Jews'?" Pilate asked cynically.

Joseph, with quiet dignity and looking straight at Pilate, replied, "Your Excellency, yes, we have come about Yeshua of Nazareth. We wish to ask a great favour of you. We would dearly like to take the body of Yeshua down from the cross before sunset."

"Is he dead already?" Pilate asked in surprise.

"Remember that he was scourged first before he was crucified," Joseph reminded Pilate who nodded, remembering that he had ordered this. Pilate was silent for a few moments.

"Excuse me for a moment," he said to his visitors and then turned to speak to Marcellus. Both Romans slowly walked away out of earshot as they discussed the request.

"What about it, Marcellus?" Pilate asked.

"Pilate, he would need to be dead, and I mean provably dead. A superficial opinion would not be enough. We can't have him recover or the authorities here will certainly cause mayhem. And you know what that means to your career."

"What do you suggest?" Pilate asked, his eyes half-closed as he carefully listened to his astute second-in-command.

"I would suggest piercing through the heart with a spear."

"Is that really necessary?" Pilate asked, his lip curling with disdain, realising that he would have to explain it to his two visitors.

"I'm afraid it is, possibly even for your own career," said Marcellus with a half-smile as they pretended to be amicably discussing the issue, well aware that the two visitors were watching closely. But despite the calculated smile, Marcellus' green eyes were cold, hard and emotionless.

"How long will I have to put up with these impossible people?" Pilate asked as he took a small parchment and wrote on it. Then he closed the parchment and put his seal on it.

"Here is your permission to take down the body," Pilate said as he finished writing. "Unfortunately we have to make sure the prophet is dead, so that will have to be done first. Do you understand?"

The two men looked at one another, fearing what this might mean. They both knew, however, that they had no other option.

"We agree, your Excellency. Thank you for your understanding," said Joseph, who took the letter from Pilate, put it in his sleeve and with a bow he and Nicodemus left the room and the palace as quickly as they could.

The gang were still at the hill where Yeshua had been crucified. They saw a group of men coming along the road from the Gennath Gate.

"Ruth, Stephen, look! It's James. Yes, and I think Joseph of Arimathea and Nicodemus Ben Gurion are with him," said Zach with eagerness.

"Joseph seems to be carrying cloths," said Stephen.

"Nicodemus seems to be carrying something too, maybe for the anointing of the body," said Ruth.

The men passed the gang and continued up the hill to where John, Yeshua's mother, and the other women remained.

Nicodemus showed a letter to the first soldier who allowed the three of them through to where the centurion was.

"Nicodemus has just passed a note to the centurion," said Stephen.

The centurion read the message from Pilate and then explained apologetically to Joseph and Nicodemus that his job was not yet finished and described what had to happen next.

"Joseph and Nicodemus seem very unhappy about something," said Ruth, watching their every move.

The centurion then said to a nearby soldier, "Get on with it, the sun is sinking and we must take down the body before sunset."

At that, one of the soldiers went to the man on the right of Yeshua and, realising that he wasn't dead, broke his legs so he could no longer lift himself to get air and would suffocate quickly. Then the soldier went to the man on Yeshua's left and, realising that he too was still alive, broke his legs.

"Did you see that?" gasped Ruth, horrified.

"How could we not see it?" answered Zach, his anger making him brusque.

The women wailed at the brutality. When the soldier arrived at the middle cross he knew that Yeshua was already dead. But to make doubly sure, as he was ordered, he took his spear and plunged it into Yeshua's chest and right up to his heart.

"Look at that! The..." Zach could hardly contain himself.

When the soldier had pierced Yeshua's heart some blood and water came out of the wound. The centurion nodded that Joseph and Nicodemus were now allowed to take the body down from the cross.

"The centurion is not happy with that Roman practice," said Stephen.

Zach was still speechless, and Ruth was swallowing hard as she clung on to him. Then, under instructions from the centurion, two soldiers came forward and lifted James up so that he could reach Yeshua's head. James slowly and most carefully disentangled the crown of thorns. Some hairs were stuck to it and it took a great deal of concentration not to pull hair from his scalp.

"It was a horrid, barbaric mess," James later told the appalled gang. He had removed the thorns one by one, though he could hardly see through his tears.

John meanwhile was removing the nails, helped by Nicodemus and another one of the soldiers. He was almost ill at the sight of Yeshua. In the end it was only his worry about Yeshua's mother that kept him going. When the crown of thorns and the nails were finally removed, the ropes holding up Yeshua were untied and his body was slowly lowered. By now the centurion and the other soldiers were helping.

When Yeshua's mother held Yeshua's body in her arms for the last time she at first seemed very composed, but then, bursting into tears, she cried out, and collapsed. John held her gently.

Joseph of Arimathea owned a tomb close by that was cut into the rock at the back of the hill where Yeshua was crucified. He had recently purchased it. So, with the body now off the cross and the nails removed, Nicodemus and Joseph, helped by James, reverently carried Yeshua's body down the hill. They were followed by John, Yeshua's mother and all the rest, including the centurion.

When they reached the bottom of the hill, the three young friends and all the rest of Yeshua's followers joined them. The cortege soon entered a little garden in front of Joseph's tomb. It was springtime, so there were some flowers there.

However, it was only Joseph, Nicodemus, and Yeshua's mother, leaning heavily on John's arm, who continued towards the square hole in the rock, marking the entrance to the tomb. There were some steps into the tomb, so Joseph and Nicodemus carefully carried the body down these and then into the tomb. Inside the entrance there was an antechamber and inside that a small room. It was in the small room that they laid Yeshua's body.

That evening John explained to Zach and his two friends that, "Nicodemus anointed Yeshua's body with the myrrh and aloes he brought. Then they wrapped the body in linen cloths, covering the head with a special cloth."

As he described the burial ritual, John's face was tense. "After they had finished," he continued, "both Nicodemus and Joseph stood there for many minutes and cried bitterly. Then they wiped away their tears, and embraced Mary, Yeshua's mother, and me. Then, as you saw, the two of them, and James and I, rolled the huge boulder over to close the tomb."

Joseph and Nicodemus stayed a little while after the burial and spoke to the people who were gathered outside the tomb. Joseph spoke first, saying, "Yes, Yeshua was undoubtedly the Messiah we have all waited for, but, sadly, many in Israel have been waiting for a different type of Messiah who, with power and might, would conquer all her enemies. Yeshua, on the other hand, was a Messiah of love and forgiveness. Tragically it took his death to convince us of that. Yeshua has told us, as clearly as anyone could, that God is our Father and loves us all uniquely and unconditionally, even if that love requires an excruciating death. And, yes, we are all sinners and need God's love and forgiveness."

With smiles and tears, the gang held each other close.

Then Nicodemus said with firm conviction but with gentleness, "Battles are short term solutions, whereas love conquers for all time. Yeshua taught us that."

"Joseph and Nicodemus seem to be really wonderful men," enthused Ruth.

"The terrible pity," said Zach, "is that there are thousands of wonderful people in Israel. Remember, we are God's people. Unfortunately, some of our leaders have been led astray by their desire for wealth and power."

Nicodemus and Joseph left after many affectionate farewells and loving words of encouragement, and began walking briskly towards the city. The sun would be setting soon and the Sabbath would begin.

CHAPTER 37

The next day, Saturday, was the Sabbath and the three spent most of the day resting, praying and reflecting on all that had happened. Zebedee's two houses in the city were full. Strange to say, everyone seemed to have accepted what had happened and a feeling of peace was in the house.

"Will Yeshua rise again, as he said he would?" asked Stephen.

"If he said he would, then he will. But I'm not sure what it means," said Ruth. "What do you think, Zach?"

"I'm not sure what it all means, but I'm sure that we'll find out fairly soon," Zach spoke confidently. Looking at him Ruth realised that he had changed. He had somehow become a man over the past few months and was much more at peace with himself, more assured.

"Do you think Yeshua will confirm for us, in some way, that there is an afterlife?" Stephen queried.

"Do you not think that he has clearly explained that to us already?" Zach replied, surprised at the question. "Yeshua was absolutely certain of it at the time the Sadducees confronted him."

"You're right, I hadn't thought of that," answered Stephen remembering this confrontation.

"Stephen, are you suggesting that Yeshua will somehow explain it all again to us even though he is dead?" Ruth asked, looking inquiringly at Stephen.

"I'm not sure what I think," replied Stephen. "Let me ask another question. Do you really think that Yeshua was the Messiah, the one our people have been waiting for, for so long?"

Zach then firmly attested, "Even without any further signs I believe that undoubtedly Yeshua was the Messiah, as Nicodemus Ben Gurion and Joseph of Arimathea said yesterday."

"And do you understand, Zach, what Yeshua meant at the Passover meal when he spoke about the bread being his body and the wine his blood?" asked Stephen.

"I think that Yeshua's body was broken for us and his blood was poured out for us, and for everyone," replied Zach with deep thoughtfulness, "but, no, I don't fully understand what he meant. I hope we will soon."

"It is beyond us all," said James with a smile tinged with sadness. "We will just have to wait patiently to find out what he meant. Our lives for the past three years, unknown to us, were a preparation for yesterday and today."

John, in the meantime, was standing looking out the window facing the street. Turning around he said, "As we all know, after the death of someone in a family, in our tradition, both friends and family are expected to attend the grave and to pray with the family for seven days, so it will be our duty, and for me a joy, to be with Mary for the duration of the feast."

The group looked at John and realised that his life was now completely changed. He had the responsibility of looking after Yeshua's mother, Mary.

"During the week many prayers are to be said and these have been laid down in our rituals. I have read them and in one we tell God of our acceptance of His will for our lives. This, therefore, will mean that we have to accept God's will for Yeshua. It will be a very difficult prayer."

He looked out the window again, wiping away tears. Then he said, "We must pray that, somehow, we will get the strength to accept everything that has happened as the will of a loving Father – a Father who has asked his special, beloved son to show us what true love really means. He told us it would be so the night before he died, the night we were not there for him."

Salome, embracing John and wiping his tears, turned to the group and said, "You heard John! We now know what we have to do. We'll stay in Jerusalem for the week of mourning with Mary."

But John was not the only one in tears. So were Zach, Stephen, Ruth and everyone else there. Zach looked at everyone and said, "Although we might feel slightly relieved that the barbaric torture is ended and Yeshua is at peace, the truth is that, in a way, we are like fishermen without their captain on a boat that is floating rudderless on an open sea. We have to ask, 'What happens when the week of mourning is over?'"

The next morning, Sunday, was the first day of the week. At a very early hour, Mary of Magdala, along with Mary of Clophas, called at Zebedee's house looking for Salome. Zach heard their soft knock and was about to go down to open the door when he saw that Salome was already there. Without noticing him, the three women gently closed the door and made their way up the town. From there they exited Jerusalem by the Gennath Gate and continued on to the tomb. Zach wasn't sure where they were going but wondered why they were up so early since everyone else was asleep. Couldn't whatever they wanted to do have waited?

Stephen appeared beside Zach. "Did I hear someone at the door?" he asked, only half-awake.

"You did. It was my mother and Mary of Magdala and Mary of Clophas," Zach said, still looking down at the door, puzzled.

"What were they doing?" asked Stephen.

"I noticed the spices in the house last night," said Zach, "but for some reason I didn't pay too much attention to them. I think that they have gone to the grave to anoint the body again, but I'm not sure."

"But Nicodemus anointed Yeshua's body... and how will they manage to remove the huge stone that is in front of the tomb?" askedStephen, now wide awake.

"I really don't know. Do you think we should go and help them?" suggested Zach.

Stephen stopped and thought for a moment, then said, "No, no need, I would say. When the sun is up we'll all be going to the tomb to pray. That's the plan for each morning of the week," Stephen smiled. "The women have their own plans. Let them at it, I say."

Zach agreed cheerfully. "You're right. They may not have gone to the tomb at all, who knows? Another hour's sleep is a better idea."

However, as Zach lay on his bed he began to imagine the three women at the tomb. 'They won't be able to move that stone,' he thought. 'Maybe I should get up and follow them after all.' But in no time he was fast asleep. The next thing he knew, he was been shaken awake. It was Stephen and Ruth. "Get up, Zach, get up!"

"What's wrong?" said Zach, sitting up in his bed, rubbing his eyes and looking at his two friends.

"Your mother and her friends were at the tomb and are back now – you need to come!" Stephen's eyes showed that there was something amiss. In no time Zach was up and on his way downstairs.

The three women were there, almost out of their minds with joy. Zach had never seen his mother so consumed with happiness and excitement. The women explained what had happened.

"When we reached the tomb, we found the stone was rolled back," said Salome, barely able to control her excitement.

"We were absolutely shocked," said Mary of Magdala in her deep voice, her hair falling loose from her haste. "Since it was open and no one was near, the three of us slowly entered the tomb. And there..."

"You won't believe it!" interrupted Mary of Clophas.

"There, inside the tomb," continued Mary of Magdala, "was a young man in white robes, sitting down on the right side of the tomb as if he had been expecting us." Mary motioned to Salome to continue.

"When we saw him we naturally screamed – who wouldn't? – we were really scared, or maybe it was fear and a strange joy mixed together," Salome suggested looking over to the other two who indicated their agreement. "We heard the young man in white say, 'Don't be alarmed, I know you are looking for Jesus of Nazareth, who was crucified. He is not here – he has been raised! Look, here is the place where he was laid.'"

"Well," continued Mary of Magdala, "we were stunned at that, not knowing what to say. But I think all three of us understood then what 'resurrection' meant. Yeshua had mentioned it many, many times in his teaching. Yes, Yeshua is, at this moment, alive. He is alive as I speak to you now. Then the young man in white added, 'Now go and give this message to his disciples, including Peter. The message is 'He is going to Galilee ahead of you; there you will see him, just as he told you.'"

Zach, Stephen and Ruth were stunned. They had a hundred questions they wanted to ask but waited as Salome continued, "The young man then stood up, smiled and was gone. He didn't go out the door or into a crevice in the tomb. We looked everywhere, he just disappeared."

Salome smiled and then said, "Zach, Stephen, Ruth! The young man was very real indeed, no doubt an angel of God. We all three of us witnessed exactly the same happening. It is true! Yeshua is alive!"

Zach anxiously asked, "Did you tell anyone in Jerusalem about this?" He was imagining what the High Priest or Pilate might do if they heard about it.

"No!" Salome said. "We met a few people we knew but told them nothing whatsoever. This is the first time we have told our story."

'Will James and John and the others believe them?' wondered Zach to himself, 'It will be interesting to see their reaction.'

There was movement at the top of the stairs. It was Mary, Yeshua's mother. She looked as if she too had had some experience that assured her that her son was alive.

"It is true," she said, "Yeshua is alive. He has risen from the dead."

When the three women who had gone to the tomb met James and John a little later in the morning the gang were with them. The women told James and John everything that had happened. But it seemed to the three friends that James and John, who were courteous and listened carefully, didn't really believe what they were hearing. John seemed a bit more open than James but both appeared doubtful. Peter then arrived and he too listened to the story. "I must see this for myself. Not that I don't believe what you say, of course, but I must go to the tomb and see it for myself."

"I'll join you," said John, and then said to the three women. "We'll be back shortly."

"I'll go with you!" said Mary of Magdala, signaling with her eyes to her two companions. They smiled conspiratorially knowing that she would make sure that Peter and John did actually go to the tomb and not just say that they had done so.

When they arrived at the tomb Peter and John went in. After looking around for a while, the down-to-earth Peter said, "This is exactly what the women described. I can't believe it. And who moved the stone? The women certainly couldn't have moved it." Peter was examining every aspect of the tomb. He even looked to see if there were any hidden ways in and out, but found nothing. The tomb was encased inside impenetrable rock. John looked carefully at the blood-stained linen cloths, which had been wrapped around Yeshua's body. They were all there, neatly folded.

"What do you make of it all, John?" asked Peter looking totally at a loss.

"I think that the women are right. Yeshua is alive. I have no idea how." John sounded both sure and unsure. "I'm sure that Yeshua will, somehow, tell us what we should do next. We will have to be patient and wait. Neither you nor I are very good at that, Peter," John pointed out. Peter smiled wryly and nodded agreement.

When the two men came out from the tomb, Mary of Magdala was outside waiting for them. "Well, isn't it true?" she asked.

"Yeshua is certainly not there," said Peter, "but as to him being alive, we will have to be patient and wait."

Peter and John hurried back to the house. They had much to report. Mary of Magdala, however, remained at the tomb. She felt a great emptiness and wondered how she could ever live without Yeshua. She began to sob. Then she decided to look in the tomb again. Slowly she made her way inside, unaware of what was about to happen.

As her eyes adjusted to the half-light, she saw two angels in front of her. Happiness radiated from them. It seemed to encompass every part of them. Despite this, she was deeply afraid. She tried to say something but found that she couldn't. Instead she just frantically rubbed the tears from her eyes to make sure that she wasn't seeing something that wasn't really there.

"Woman, why are you weeping?" one of the angels asked her kindly.

"They have taken my Lord away and I do not know where they have put him," she replied, having found the words. The angels, however, seemed to be looking at something outside the tomb. She turned to see what it was but she only saw a gardener. When she looked back, the angels were gone. Her mind was in turmoil. What now? Where have they gone? She didn't know what to do or think. Finally, she decided to talk to the gardener.

As she neared him, her heart almost stopped. She thought she was going mad. She shook her head and looked again at the gardener's face.

"Mary," he said with a loving smile. It was Yeshua.

"Teacher," she replied, stunned, and fell to her knees.

She took hold of his feet, fearing that he would disappear or that somehow she was in a trance. But Yeshua told her affectionately not to hold on to him since he had not yet ascended to his Father, and that she should go and tell the 'brothers' that, "I am returning to him who is my Father and their Father, my God and their God."

She looked into his eyes and then... he was gone. She stood up, looked right and left but he was nowhere to be seen. 'What will I do now?' she asked herself. 'Nobody will believe me.'

She laughed at her predicament but was filled with joy and thanks. 'Yeshua has appeared to me, to me,' she said to herself over and over.

When Mary told the women what had happened they didn't need convincing, they were quite sure that everything she said was true. She was delighted at their response. Then, seeing the gang and knowing how much all of this meant to them, she decided to tell them before she told the Eleven.

"We believe you, Mary," Zach assured her, and his statement was confirmed by the nods from Ruth and Stephen.

The Eleven, however, after discussing the story amongst themselves, considered the whole incident impossible — just the fantasies of a woman overwrought with grief.

"Esther, Sarah and I feel that we should return to Capernaum to do what the angel announced," said Salome talking to the gang. "You remember, what he said about Yeshua, 'He is going to Galilee ahead of you; there you will see him, just as he told you.'"

"That's a great idea," said Ruth, as Zach and Stephen signalled their agreement.

"Right," said Salome, "We will begin our journey after noon today."

Zach, Ruth and Stephen excitedly began to make preparations for the trip.

Two hours later, as they were about to leave, Zach saw two well-dressed, elderly men making their way towards the house. Zach stepped back into the hallway and said, "Joseph of Arimathea and Nicodemus Ben Gurion are coming down the street. I think they are coming to our house."

When the two visitors arrived it was Nicodemus who spoke. "Both Joseph and I are leaving the city today and we just heard that you too, Salome, Esther and Sarah, are on your way back to Capernaum. Both Joseph and I would dearly like to join you. As you can understand, both of us need time to consider what has happened and what the future holds for us. Happily, members of both our families live in Tiberius. We hope to stay with them for a while."

"We would be delighted if you would travel with us," Salome said. She knew that her companions and the gang would love nothing more.

Within the hour they were all on their way.

During their six-day journey to Galilee the gang and their mothers were delighted to share what they had experienced during the three years with Yeshua, the great moments and the moments of confrontation and fear. The two dignitaries from Jerusalem listened very carefully and discussed many issues with them.

"And do you believe that Yeshua is alive?" asked Stephen.

"Yes! We both do," said Nicodemus with great certainty.

"Stephen, there is nothing more certain," Joseph added with conviction.

With all their connections throughout both Judea and Galilee, Joseph and Nicodemus were able to arrange accommodation each night. However, their journey together came to an end when they reached Tiberius, where Salome, Esther and Sarah and the gang were very sorry to have to say goodbye.

"It has been a delight to be with you," said Nicodemus. "Both Joseph and I have learned a great deal from you all. And gang, never underestimate how fortunate you have been to be friends of Yeshua of Nazareth, the Messiah. Remember he will always look after you in a very special way."

"Thank you so much for being with us on the journey," Salome said, gratefully embracing the departing men. All the others did likewise.

As they were leaving Salome added, "We are only a few miles away. You will always be welcome at Capernaum."

They all waved goodbye and, travelling on with raised spirits, they could hardly wait to get home. The gang wondered whether Capernaum would have changed since they left.

CHAPTER 38

When the gang and Salome arrived home, Zebedee was just coming in from fishing. There had been good catches since they had left and business was going well. As soon as Zebedee saw them he went to a container of water, washed his hands and came quickly over to them. Throwing his arms around Salome he said, "It's wonderful to have you back! But you are here much sooner than expected. I didn't think you'd be here for another six days or so. Is everything all right? Did everything go well?" He looked into Salome's eyes and over at Zach to see if he could uncover the reason for their early arrival.

Salome answered, "It's wonderful to be back, Zebedee, and we are all safe and sound, including James and John. At least they were fine when we left them. But we have so much to tell you."

Ruth, after greeting Zebedee, and saying a special goodbye to Zach, went home with her mother to tell their family all about Yeshua and their pilgrimage to Jerusalem. Stephen and his mother also hurried home. They too couldn't wait to tell the family everything they had experienced during their time away.

Zebedee turned to his workers and signalled to them to continue with the work and that he was finished for the day. They smiled and waved at Salome and Zach.

That evening and over the next few days, Salome and Zach told Zebedee in detail everything that happened since they had left Capernaum.

"Considering all the problems Yeshua had with the teachers of the Law," Zebedee said, "and the Pharisees and the visitors from Jerusalem, I am not at all surprised that they found a way to get rid of him. I am sorry about Judas though. I always found him a very competent person and easy to deal with. Life is strange. As for Yeshua being alive! I am willing to accept that too because someone who can dictate to the winds and waves as he did on our Sea of Galilee must certainly be able to overcome death."

"Ruth, life somehow seems different now that we have returned home. What do you think?" asked Zach, some days later, sitting beside the lake, looking at the constant ebb and flow of the small waves.

"Yes. All of us who went to Jerusalem have been changed by what happened there. Our whole way of thinking about life and its meaning is different now," Ruth replied as she watched a bird dive into the water looking for food.

"Each night, now, as I am going to sleep, I wonder if I will ever be able to settle down and live a normal life again," said Zach looking over at Ruth again.

"I feel exactly the same, Zach. I ask myself 'what next?'" She shrugged her shoulders.

"There's Stephen. Let's see what he feels about our future here." Zach stood up and caught Stephen's eye. He came over immediately and sat down beside them.

"Stephen, Ruth and I have been talking about how difficult it is to settle back here in Capernaum now. How are you finding it?"

"Well actually, I found out today that I won't be settling here in Capernaum. My dad has been posted to Jerusalem and we'll be leaving in about two months. The question now is whether or not I will be able settle down in Jerusalem. I doubt if I will settle anywhere ever again. At least that is how I feel right now. I am actually considering asking Peter, James, John and the rest if I could join them in passing on the teaching of Yeshua in Jerusalem. Somehow I feel that this is what I am supposed to do." Stephen looked uncertainly at both Zach and Ruth to see how they were taking this.

"Stephen," said Zach enthusiastically, "I think that you'd be an excellent person to pass on Yeshua's teachings. Not many people understand his message like you do. And know the Scriptures like you do. I think that you are cut out to be an ambassador for Yeshua. What do you think, Ruth?"

"I agree entirely with Zach," she said. "Stephen, ever since I met you I felt that your future was to be a teacher of God's ways. And now we understand God's ways much better, you will be able to teach them as Yeshua taught them. No better person to do it, in my view."

Stephen gazed at both his friends, his eyes brimming with tears. "Thank you," Stephen quietly said. "Thank you."

Two weeks passed and Zach was back at work. "I am beginning to love this whole way of life again, but in a deeper kind of way," he told his dad. "I love the boats, the sails, the sound of the water, the wind, the waves, the expectation of a catch, the shoals of fish filling our nets and the many, many moments of just being there and being alive. When I get moments of quiet I feel really content just slowly reciting some of my favourite psalms or being in silence with God within my inner self. I am also sure that Yeshua is in God, as God was in him in a special way when he was with us."

"You have changed, Zach," said Zebedee. "You have changed in very many ways since being with Yeshua."

Two days later the Zebedee household had a celebratory meal for the return of James and John. The families of Stephen and Ruth were invited to the supper. Simon Peter, Andrew, Joseph and the rest of the Eleven had gone to Bethsaida.

Even though James and John were still tired, they recounted everything that had happened in Jerusalem since Salome and the gang had left to come home.

"The first news we have for you is very sad ... Judas is dead," James said. "He had bought a field with the money he received for betraying Yeshua, but before he was able to do anything with it he died tragically. Some said he killed himself. Anyway, everyone in Jerusalem heard about it and the field he bought has been named the 'Field of Blood' – a terrible name."

Zach said thoughtfully, "I'm sure that Yeshua has forgiven him, because deep-down Judas was a good man who just made bad decisions and was wrong about what God wanted."

"I agree," said Stephen supportively.

"We will all pray for him," said Salome, "God is good."

Then James and John gave the group a step by step account of their week in Jerusalem.

"The Temple veil that marked off the sanctuary area was torn apart the very moment Yeshua died!" said John. "We only found that out later. Poor Caiaphas was at his wit's end to explain how it had happened."

John took a cup of water, slowly sipped it and then continued, "You already know what took place at the tomb early on Sunday morning." Salome smiled when he said that. "However," John continued, "something else amazing happened that day around sunset." John gestured to James, who continued the story.

"We, the Eleven, were rather skeptical, I have to admit, about Yeshua being alive and appearing to people," James said, "although John seemed to have accepted Yeshua's resurrection after his visit to the tomb. Well, that evening, John was proven right.

"The sun was about thirty minutes from setting when out of nowhere Yeshua appeared among us. All around the room were gasps of disbelief. And there is no doubt that the door of the house was securely locked against intruders. Peter stood up immediately, when he saw him, only to hear Yeshua say, 'Peace be with you.'

"Well, Peter didn't know how to respond. He, like me, was overcome with a whole mixture of emotions. Then a number of the others stood up, but they took steps back from Yeshua."

John put his arm around James' shoulder and continued, "Yeshua, knew how upset, and even afraid, some of us were, but he showed us his hands and his feet so that no one could deny that it was he who was there with us. Then he said again, 'Peace be with you. As the Father sent me, so I send you.' And he breathed on us and said, 'Receive the Holy Spirit. If you forgive people's sins, they are forgiven; if you do not forgive them, they are not forgiven.'"

James smiled but with a certain sadness. He shook his head and said, "I still feel ashamed of letting Yeshua down in the garden. Perhaps we could have prevented the whole crucifixion if we hadn't already decided that Yeshua was invincible."

"But, James," said John, looking into his brother's eyes, "Yeshua *is* invincible. It was he himself who decided to die. Yes, we messed up badly, but in the end it was his heavenly Father, God, who asked Yeshua to die as he did, and no one could divert Yeshua from fulfilling that request. His dreadful death showed us, in ways that we can only begin to understand, how much God loves humankind and to what lengths he will go for us."

"Did Yeshua appear again to anyone else?" It was Elizabeth, Zach's second youngest sister who asked the question.

"Yes he did," said John. "You see the first time Yeshua appeared to us Thomas 'the twin' was not there in the room with the rest of us and when he heard what had happened he was very, very slow to believe our story. He told us all, 'Unless I see the scars of the nails in his hands and put my finger on those scars and my hand into his side, I will not believe it.'

Then, exactly a week later, Yeshua came into the room once more, and again the door was firmly locked. He repeated his original greeting to us, 'Peace be with you.' But this time he turned to Thomas and quietly said, 'Thomas, put your finger here, and look at my hands. Then reach out your hand and put it in my side. Stop your doubting, and believe!'

Thomas was speechless and could hardly move. He stared at Yeshua. And then, very slowly, he stretched over and did just what Yeshua had asked him to do. Then he fell on his knees and said, 'My Lord and my God.'

Yeshua asked him, 'Do you believe because you see me? How happy are those who believe without seeing me.'

Thomas was now satisfied that Yeshua was really alive and at the same time you could see he was sorry for being so slow to believe us.

Yeshua stayed a little while and then left just as he had come. No one had any idea how."

James and John continued their stories and everyone wanted to hear more and more. They told the story of the two followers of Yeshua who were really downhearted after the crucifixion and, having left Jerusalem, were on their way back to Emmaus. Yeshua had joined them as they walked along.

"They listened to him but still didn't recognize him," explained John. "However, they were so delighted with the man's understanding of the whole meaning of the Scriptures and how the Scriptures referred to what had just happened in Jerusalem, that they invited the man to stay with them for a meal, not knowing who he was. But as the man broke bread with them, they recognised that it was Yeshua. Then, as he had come, so he had gone. They had no idea where he went. What would you do, Elizabeth, if that happened to you?" asked John.

Elizabeth looked up at John and then put her hand under her chin as she considered the question. "I think I would go and tell Peter what happened," she suggested. "The people in the house where they were staying would probably not understand what they were talking about."

John laughed and then looked at his young sister with great admiration. "You are a smart one, Elizabeth, because that is exactly what they did."

Elizabeth and her sister, who was lying on the ground beside her, were delighted at the attention and congratulations they were receiving from their big brother.

"So, as Elizabeth suggested, the two men immediately got up from the table and ran the whole way back to Jerusalem to tell the rest of us."

John at that stage motioned to his dad that it was getting late.

"I think it's time for bed for you two," said Zebedee to his young daughters. At first they weren't too pleased but in the end they said goodnight and went off to bed.

"Thank you so much for your stories," said Salome, very proud of her two sons. "The meaning of Yeshua's life becomes all the more clear as time passes."

Then both Stephen's family, and Ruth's family joined in and said that they were absolutely sure that Yeshua was the Messiah – or, as Ruth's mother clarified, "Yeshua *is* the Messiah."

Chapter 39

Over the next number of days most of the Eleven visited the Zebedee house at various times. They were discussing things together a great deal, trying to decide what they would do next. Yeshua, as John explained earlier to his parents, had instructed the Eleven to 'Go and teach all nations.'

"But how can we fulfil this wish?" worried John. "That is our problem."

One late afternoon, however, when Peter was visiting the Zebedee house, Bartholomew and Thomas the twin were there. Peter announced that he was considering going fishing through the night and that he would be delighted to have some company.

"When I am out in the sea fishing, I find I can think more clearly. The fresh air seems to invigorate me. I really need to make acquaintance with the sea again," he said.

Zebedee smiled. Peter was putting into words how he, Zebedee, also felt about fishing and the sea.

"Peter," said James, "John and I would be delighted to join you tonight. What about you Zach?"

Zach was chuffed that James could suggest that he too should go. "I would love to go," said Zach and then looked at Joseph, "but I would also like Joseph to come too if you have room for both of us."

"I was banking on Joseph coming," said Peter, "but now that more of you want to come I will take out the bigger boat so there will be plenty of room for everyone."

"In that case, Peter, I would also love to join you. I could do with some time in the fresh air." It was Thomas who spoke. Peter was delighted.

"If Thomas can survive it, I suppose so can I," said Bartholomew immediately with his usual, happy laugh.

"Great," said Peter, as he stood up, glad to be going fishing again. "I will be at the jetty as soon as I can."

A short time later, everyone was aboard Peter's boat ready to spend the night fishing. There was a breeze and as the boat cut through the water Zach turned to Joseph and said, "Being here in the boat reminds me so much of our days with Yeshua."

"I can't get Yeshua out of my mind," confided Joseph, "I really miss him. So does Simon, or Peter, as he is now called. He told me about his denial in the courtyard and finds it hard to forgive himself."

Zach realised that Joseph was very affected by his big brother's failure. "Well, let me tell you, Joseph. All of us would have done the same thing. Peter was, in fact, extremely brave. Firstly, he tried to defend Yeshua in the garden, but Yeshua told him to put away his sword. Next, he, without thought for himself, followed Yeshua, despite all the clubs and swords of the mob. Then he went into the courtyard of the palace. Very, very few would have taken the risks that he took. It could easily have spelt death for him. That night, the tension was so high, so high. Everyone knew that what was happening was unlawful. So, if anyone had admitted to knowing Yeshua or being a companion of his, who knows what would have happened to them? No, and I am sure of this, just after your brother had said that he didn't know Yeshua, I saw Yeshua looking at him. Yeshua knew what had happened, and yet the look I saw was a look of love. I am sure of that. Stephen was there too, he agrees completely with what I am saying. There is every reason to be enormously proud of your brother. I would be."

Joseph, normally so outgoing, was holding back a sob. He held Zach's hand and said, "Thank you, Zach, I actually am very proud of my brother, but he needs to forgive himself."

Zach nodded his understanding. But just then the wind turned and they were both required to help. Unfortunately, that night they didn't catch a single fish, but just being on the sea helped them to put aside, for a while, the many problems they faced.

"Time to go home," said Peter, "better fishing next time."

Soon daylight began to appear. But as Zach glanced towards the shore he noticed that there was someone standing there. He had no idea who it was. But the person on the shore called out across the water,

"Young men, haven't you caught anything?"

"Not a thing," shouted Joseph, tidying up some bits and pieces.

"Throw your net out on the right side of the boat, and you will catch some," the person on the shore suggested.

Peter shook his head. Surely he would know as well as anyone where the fish would be at any particular time, probably better than most of the fishermen in the area, if not in all Galilee. He later couldn't explain why he did it, but he threw out the net once again.

"Now, what… 'Mister Stranger'?" Peter mumbled as he put his arms on his hips, studying the nets. Then to his complete astonishment he saw the nets begin to fill with fish.

"How did he know the fish were there?" Peter muttered. "And where have they all come from? We've been in this area all night."

Then Joseph gave Zach a dig in the arm and whispered, "I believe that that is Yeshua on the shore."

Zach looked again, this time more carefully and, yes, indeed it was Yeshua. He was about to shout out, but John beat him to it.

"It is the Lord!" shouted John joyfully.

Peter held on to the mast and looked at the shore, 'It couldn't be,' he said to himself. But after a moment he realized that John was right. Immediately, Peter got his outer garment and put it on, jumped into the water and began wading towards Yeshua. The water wasn't deep, though the boat was still some distance from the shore. James took over as skipper and the others stayed in the boat dragging in a net that was, by then, almost bursting with fish.

As they came closer to the shore, Zach remarked, "Look, Joseph, Yeshua has bread already prepared for everyone and has a charcoal fire burning with fish cooking on it."

"And see, my family, your family, and yes, Ruth's family and Stephen's family have arrived. This is extraordinary!" Joseph's whole face lit up as he looked at the number of people gathered for 'Yeshua's breakfast'.

Zach just shook his head, though he felt like shouting out for joy.

As he was tying up the boat and pulling in all the fish, his two sisters ran over to the boat. Zach looked up and saw them coming and behind them was Ruth. The two sisters spoke at once, "Yeshua is here, Zach!"

"She likes you, Zach," Esther, the younger sister observed, looking over at Ruth. Elizabeth, the older sister, smiled and linked Ruth's arm.

Zach, meanwhile, put Esther on his shoulders and the four of them walked as briskly as they could towards their families.

Salome met them just before they arrived and smilingly asked if they could collect some fish from the catch since more were needed for the breakfast. She also suggested that the two young sisters might first count the fish. Ruth winked at Salome and said that she and Zach would go with them to help. They were soon down at the boat where two of Peter's men had laid out the fish. Immediately, they began counting. After a few minutes they were finished.

"How many did you count, Esther?" asked Zach.

"I think there are one-hundred-and-fifty-three there. Am I right?" She wasn't certain.

So with help from Elizabeth and Ruth she counted them all again.

"You were right the first time!" congratulated Ruth.

Soon they were walking back briskly. Zach said, "I am absolutely sure that this catch is an all-time record for the Sea of Galilee." His sisters cheered loudly.

By the time they arrived back and handed over eight big fish, everyone was in great form. Yeshua was moving from group to group greeting people. He had words for everyone including, of course, Simon Peter, Bartholomew and Thomas, and also for all the parents, and each member of the gang. However, the time passed quickly and it wasn't long before Yeshua had blessed the exultant group and then, somehow, was no longer with them.

Everyone was extremely happy to have spent this time with Yeshua, but they also felt sure that it was the last time they would see him.

For a few hours the group stood around and discussed what had just taken place. Peter said that at one stage during the breakfast, Yeshua had taken him aside. "He asked me three times whether I really loved him. After I had said I did three times, I realised that he was showing me that my denying him three times in Jerusalem was totally forgiven."

"But of course you are completely forgiven, Peter," said Salome.

"He also asked me to take charge of his work into the future," Peter said with great humility. "Yeshua said, 'Take care of my lambs and sheep.'"

"Who better?" said Zebedee. Everyone agreed.

Later, Peter told James and John that Yeshua told him that he, Peter, would be badly treated later in life. "I was not surprised," said Peter quietly to James and John. "In fact, I was delighted to be asked by Yeshua to show some love through suffering. That will be a huge gift."

"You are absolutely right, Peter, but how many of us would have said that before we met Yeshua?" said John. James agreed.

That evening the same group met again in the Zebedee house and each one recounted what Yeshua had personally said to him or her. Joseph recalled how Yeshua had said that he must remember the poor always. "Before Yeshua came along I never gave much thought to the poor in our area, but now I realise that poor people are very special to God. Yeshua explained that to me that what I do for poor people I do for him." Peter looked with approval at his young brother.

When it came to Stephen's turn he, though abashed, quietly shared, "Yeshua told me that he wanted me to spread his message of the kingdom in Jerusalem. He also said that my life would be short and that I would have many difficulties to contend with there... I feel so privileged that Yeshua chose me for that work."

When Stephen finished telling his story people hardly knew what to say. The three other gang members realised that this was the moment for a hug from them. Then everyone started applauding. Stephen just stood there with tears in his eyes. This time they were tears of joy.

At that stage everyone had spoken except Zach and Ruth. They had kept very quiet, hoping that they wouldn't have to speak.

"And what about Zach and Ruth?" asked Salome.

"Yes," said Stephen, who was delighted that the focus was now off him. So Zach began, "When Yeshua turned to Ruth and me," Zach revealed, "he smiled and looked at both of us with great love. I realised then that a whole new way of life was ahead of us. After three years journeying with Yeshua, my life has changed. A loving God has replaced a silly and wrong idea of God in my heart. Yeshua's death clearly showed us that. And, Yeshua is alive! Death is not the end."

He then added, "I have said too much. But I must announce this. I hope to study medicine for a few years, and after that I would be so happy if Ruth and I could spread Yeshua's message together. Yeshua's caring smile seemed to suggest that that was the future for us and I can think of nothing more wonderful... if she will have me."

Zach turned to Ruth.

Ruth began to blush. But after a few moments, with a gentle smile, she faced the room,

"Since being with Yeshua," she said, "I feel that all our thoughts and ideas about life have changed in so many ways. After a few years of study," she continued, "I would be truly honoured to spend the rest of my life with Zach. Like Zach, I feel that Yeshua did suggest that both Zach and I could together spread Yeshua's message of love and caring." Ruth turned and looked at Zach. "In truth, I would be lost without Zach," she declared.

Then Stephen and Joseph went over to Zach and Ruth and now the gang stood together. It was Ruth who began the singing,

"Let us praise the Lord the God of Israel! He has come to the help of His people and has set them free."

Lightning Source UK Ltd.
Milton Keynes UK
UKOW03f1226050617
302705UK00002B/195/P